Petty
Pain

Understanding the Assignment of Offense

Margo Wright Williams

Harmony Series

Unless otherwise indicated, all Scripture quotations are taken from the *Holy Bible*, New King James Version, copyright© 1982.

Scripture quotations marked KJV are from the King James Version of the Bible, copyright 1982.

Scripture quotations marked NIV are from the New International Version, copyright 1984.

Scripture quotations marked NLT are from the New Living Translation of the Bible, copyright 1996, 2004, 2007.

Edited by Tamika L. Sims, Get Write With Tamika

Cover by Perfect Designx.

PETTY PAIN: UNDERSTANDING THE ASSIGNMENT OF OFFENSE

Copyright ©2020 by Margo W. Williams

Published by Graceful Fire Publishing

PO Box 1361

Irmo, South Carolina 29063

www.margowwilliams.org

Library of Congress Catalog Control Number: 2020904517

ISBN: 978-1-7346585-0-7

All rights reserved. No part of this publication may be reproduced, stored in a retrieval system, or transmitted in any form or by any means – electronic, mechanical, digital, photocopy, recording, or any other – except for brief quotations in printed reviews, without the prior permission of the publisher.

Printed in the United States of America

Dedicated to Lee A. Williams, my beloved husband and soul mate. I thank him for his tireless love, endless support, and inspiring humor. He is the iron that sharpens the blade of my being.

To our beautiful children, Mattison and Morgan, their lives are the impetus of my focus.

Our soul has escaped as a bird from the snare of the fowlers; the snare is broken, and we have escaped. Our help is in the name of the LORD, Who made heaven and earth.

~ Psalm 124:7-8

Contents

Foreword by Dr. Katrina Hutchins ix

Foreword by Dr. Garry James xi

Preface xiii

Introduction xvii

Part One: The EVENT

Chapter 1: What is Offense? 3
  John 16:1
Chapter 2: Garden Offense 15
  Galatians 5:7-8

Part Two: The POSITION

Chapter 3: Anatomy of Offense 25
  1 John 2:10
Chapter 4: The Pathology of Offense 43
  Psalm 51:6
Chapter 5: Symptoms 51
  2Corinthians 4:18
Chapter 6: Forgiveness 61
  Matthew 18:33
Chapter 7: TRAPS 71
  Psalm 124:7
  Psalm 139:23
Chapter 8: The Spirit of Offense 91
  Philippians 1:9-10

Part Three: The CHANGE

Chapter 9: Reconciliation 107
    2Corinthians 5:18

Chapter 10: Maturity 121
    Galatians 5:22-23

Chapter 11: Response 133
    Romans 15:5

Chapter 12: Wounded Soul 147
    Psalm 23:3

Chapter 13: Working Together 157
    Romans 8:28

Chapter 14: Biblical Examples 167
    2Timothy 3:16

Chapter 15: A Treasury of Testimonies 177
    Revelation 12:11

Chapter 16: Scripture Tools 193
    Psalm 18:28

Afterword 199
Appendix A 201
Appendix B 203
Appendix C 205
Appendix D 207
Appendix E 209
Appendix F 213
About the Author 215

Foreword

I am fascinated by some of the newest television shows that bring the viewer up-close and personal with surgeries of various kinds. There are surgeries for weight loss, surgeries on feet and surgeries to enhance various body parts. I am intrigued by them all. However, my favorite show is, "Dr. Pimple Popper."

The show begins with a warning regarding the graphic content that will be shown. In each segment, viewers are introduced to patients who have been plagued with extreme growths of various sorts and sizes. They come to see the doctor because the growth has impeded their lives in some way and/or rendered them dysfunctional. The Dr. has earned the reputation as an expert at identifying and diagnosing the growths, cutting them open and allowing the contents to ooze out or be extracted. After her procedures, without fail, patients leave the physician's office, freed from the growth and on the path to healing.

How does "Dr. Pimple Popper" relate to this book? Well, I am glad you asked! In *Petty Pain*, author Margo W. Williams has assumed a role as physician and surgeon. With strategic precision, she has identified and diagnosed "offense" as a toxic growth many of us are carrying and one that is killing us silently. In every chapter and with great care, she has crafted her writing to be the scalpel she uses to cut open the malignant growths that have invaded the hearts, minds and spirits of people...God's people.

Cutting through excuses, unforgiveness, grudges, anger, betrayal and other deep wounds, this book is the surgical instrument God has anointed for the purpose of setting His people free from the entrapment of offense. The book also serves as a guide, leading us into a greater understanding of the cause, the symptoms and the pathology of offense.

While the book does not end with the assurance you will never be offended again, it does end with the keen recognition that there is a Doctor in the house.

Dr. Katrina Hutchins
President/CEO of Re-Source Solutions

Author of, *The Voice Positioning System: 7 Ways to Harness Your Power and Master Your Influence*

Foreword

One of the most challenging times that a follower of Christ will face in their walk with the Lord is when they experience what many Christians call "church hurt." These experiences occur when Christians are harmed emotionally and spiritually by other Christians. Church hurt typically catches believers off guard as they are immediately faced with the decision to be stymied by the treatment of others or to be an overcomer in every sense of the Word.

Margo Williams has provided prayerful insight into the challenges and potential triumphs that are a part of this dynamic. Rev. Williams has prayerfully crafted a resource that could potentially save believers months, even years, of spiritual agony by leaning on the everlasting arms of the Lord to use these experiences as life lessons that not only motivate, but propel the reader toward the trajectory that the Lord intended for their lives. We celebrate this phenomenal work by one of God's faithful servants and pray that it brings glory to our King!

Dr. Garry James
Staff Developer & Training Director

Author of *Drying Silent Tears*

Preface

The Spirit of offense has worked in mankind since the beginning because whenever people are involved, there is an opportunity for someone to be hurt. Jesus was clear when He said, *"It's impossible for us not to be offended."*[1] In other words, He was leveling the playing field by reminding us that offense is common within relationships. We were created to have relationships with others and by design, our associations are to provoke growth in one another. The Bible uses the imagery of *"iron sharpening iron"* to emphasize the power of having rapport with others.[2]

> *"As iron sharpens iron, so a man sharpens the countenance of his friend."*
>
> ~ Proverbs 27:17 NKJV

Having to deal with others in proximity potentially has a way of changing us. We can either become better, bitter or blasé. When life happens, we can look back in regret, all the while unable to change anything that has occurred. Others will stoically deny the impact of the incident intending to move on from the past. However, when you choose to embrace the now, it means you pause to assess the damages while reconstructing the accident, with a hope of learning how to reduce the probability of the same thing happening again. Mother Teresa said, "Yesterday is gone. Tomorrow has not yet come. We have only today. Let us begin."

Few dare to accept the challenge because dealing with offense requires the confrontation of factors both within and outside the

---

[1] Luke 17:1
[2] Proverbs 27:17

thick layers of self: self-will, personal-strength, and self-righteousness. I am a witness to the power of relationships to change your life. My personal experiences have served to teach me the areas of my life, which needed to grow and those that should die or be pruned. The Master Gardener is very skillful in knowing how to locate the deepest roots of the greenest gardens. This book is birthed out of my personal testimony and many years of ministering to those who battle the daily consequences of remaining in offense to the words, attitudes, looks and schemes of others.

Far too many times, I have grieved as I listened and watched a display of pettiness between relatives, friends, co-workers, neighbors, church members and spouses. It is undeniable that the pain is authentic, but the source is not credible. Petty pain is a direct result of a lack of genuine love, knowledge and self-control. When these areas are properly harnessed in our lives, we become equipped to overcome and withstand the unfortunate premeditated and unintended actions toward us.

As I continue to grow in the grace of Jesus Christ, I acknowledge that dealing with offense has been one of the greatest and most powerful challenges of my faith. In some instances, I was offended and at other times, I was the offender. Both positions require the supernatural power of the Holy Spirit to be at work. God placed me in some environments, which forced me to face the dreaded issue of negative confrontation. In my quest to be the "nice Christian," on occasion, I succumbed to the snare of the enemy to incarcerate my person, out of fear of retaliation and erroneous doctrines. I also learned that my "nice Christian" nature was fueled by His grace working in my life. The same grace empowered me to confront wickedness, be a voice for the mute, to stand alone in what I know to be righteous, and to walk through the flames of humiliation, judgment and betrayal. The resulting lesson is that offense has the power to exponentially increase or decrease your spiritual life. God is strategic in *"perfecting the areas that concern us,"* therefore it is imperative for us to take daily inventory of our ways so that we can grow and mature.

> *"The Lord will perfect that which concerns me: your mercy, O LORD, endures forever: forsake not the works of your own hands."*
>
> ~ Psalm 138:8 NKJV

Prophetic Warning

Jesus foretold that the increase of offense is one sign of the last days. He said, *"And then many will be offended, will betray one another, and will hate one another"* (Matt 24:10 NKJV). When a person is offended, he becomes vulnerable to lies. Jesus warned that in the last days false prophets would *"rise up and deceive many"* (Matt 24:11 NKJV). People have turned their backs on their families, friends and the churches, because of being offended. Many Christians have ignored offense because they don't understand how detrimental it can be to their soul. Unfortunately for some, when they have asked for advice, they have received worldly counsel instead of biblical truth.

The outcome of this writing is to disturb your spiritual conscience enough to motivate you to a deeper, more rewarding relationship with the Lord and with one another. If you find that you are carrying offense with anyone in your life, use these words as inspiration and instruction to initiate the healing and restoration needed.

Introduction

Offense is not only what happened to you. It is mostly how you process and respond that determines your healing. You will either stay in the valley or go to the mountain top. I suggest you keep moving. God can heal you no matter where you find yourself. He is the Lily in the Valley, but He has also met many that were offended, on the mountain.

Offenses can cause you to go on defense and before you know it, you are stuck, no longer moving forward. You can unconsciously become more focused on protecting and preserving yourself than progressing by attacking life. Many have scored so few points towards their life's purpose and others have left the game completely and vowed never to return. However, God is asking …what did I call you to do?

Margo, my loving wife of 31 years, has been truly led to get her readers and listeners to a position of "consciously competent" with their offenses. Only then can you max out your life, move forward and multiply.

Lee A. Williams
National Sales Director

Contributing author of *True Wealth Starts in the Mind*

petty
adjective

/ˈpet̬·i/

1. small or of little importance
2. not important and not worth giving attention to[3]

pain
noun

/peɪn/

1. a bad or unpleasant physical feeling, often caused by injury or illness, that you want to stop, or an emotional feeling of this type
2. a feeling of physical suffering caused by injury or illness
3. emotional or mental suffering[4]

---

[3] https://dictionary.cambridge.org/us/dictionary/english/petty
[4] https://dictionary.cambridge.org/us/dictionary/english/pain

Part One
The
EVENT

"A thing that happens or takes place, especially one of importance."

~ Oxford Dictionary

What has happened?

"Therefore, let us not judge one another anymore, but rather resolve this, not to put a stumbling block or a cause to fall in our brother's way."

~ Romans 14:13 NKJV

Have you ever counted the number of times in each day that you said, "Excuse me" or "Please forgive me?" We have all found ourselves in situations where the practice of old-fashioned courtesy could solve the dilemma. Perhaps you are the one who offers the courtesy and it does not appear to be reciprocated towards you. You may even be wondering why you feel so obligated to smooth things over. Or, how can others so easily dismiss their rudeness? In either scenario, the fundamental responsibility remains with self. A single incident which causes injury, harm, or hurt feelings, is an offense. The cost of the offense is determined by its weight in your life. Whether it is a one-time situation or every now and then, offenses have the potential to heal or destroy. Paul advised the church in Rome to consider themselves and make a conscious decision to not be a hindrance in another's life. That one-time, single incident is merely an event.

Chapter 1
What is Offense?

"These things I have spoken to you, that you should not be made to stumble."

~ John 16:1 NKJV

When our adversary held his position in Heaven, he was a decorated angel. The Bible describes him as being arrayed in precious stones, which released a sound of worship as he moved. He was living in the brilliance of the magnificence of our Lord. He had everything; he was with God day and night. Ezekiel records God as saying that Lucifer was *"the seal of perfection, full of wisdom and perfect in beauty"* (Ez 28:12 NKJV). He was not acquainted with sickness, defeat, or hatred; pure light and love was the culture in Heaven.

As we study God's Word, we should be able to discern a divine relationship between the essence of our being and the name we are called. This relationship is often prophetic in nature or is indicative of a shift in position or character. We see the name change with Abraham and Sarah, his wife. When they began their journey from Ur, they were known as Abram and Sarai. Prior to the promise, Abram's given name meant "father exalted," and Sarai's name meant "princess" and "she that strives." God literally changed their names as a sign of their purpose. The established covenant meant that Abraham was to become *"the father of a multitude,"* and Sarah's destiny was to be *"mother of nations"* (Gen 17:16 NKJV). Isaac, her promised child, was a fulfilment of prophecy; he is revered as the second of the three patriarchs of Israel. Consequently, Lucifer's character of "morning star" was exchanged for Satan, the "adversary."

> *"How you are fallen from heaven, O Lucifer, son of the morning! How you are cut down to the ground, you who weakened the nations!"*
>
> ~ Isaiah 14:12 NKJV

Despite Heaven's splendor, darkness filled his heart. *"You were perfect in your ways from the day that you were created, until iniquity was found in you"* (Ez 28:15 NKJV). There are times we are unable to see the value in all the Lord has provided for us and when it is taken away, we become resentful. It is common to undervalue what we don't have the capacity to honor. Lucifer was not satisfied with possessing a beauty only God could grant. He was offended at God.

In my imagination, I believe Lucifer was in position to be an example to us in two ways. First, he lived in the presence of God. This is an astonishing truth. We have yet to realize the breathtaking aura of being in Heaven. We worship and pray, but we cannot imagine the divine state of being in the Heavenly presence of the Creator of Heaven and earth. Reading the pages of our Bible, we can merely catch a glimmer of Heaven's radiance. The Ancient of Days had given him the best of everything, so he lacked nothing!

Second, he didn't appreciate the gift of God in his life. Rather than being grateful that he lived in the domain of unrestricted blessings; a cold and callous heart reeking of pride was being cultivated. He desired what did not belong to him; he wanted to be like God. He wanted the glory of God to be thrust upon him. The Lord removed him from Heaven to earth. Sadly, we often fail to recognize and value the presence of God in our lives. The Scripture describes a continuous state of joy for those who are conscious of His existence. Not only does God want us to acknowledge His presence, He wants us to reverence Him.

> *"For you have said in your heart: 'I will ascend into heaven, I will exalt my throne above the stars of God, I will also sit on the mount of the congregation on the farthest sides of the*

north; I will ascend above the heights of the clouds, I will be like the Most High.' Yet you shall be brought down to Sheol, to the lowest depths of the Pit."

~ Isaiah 14:13-15 NKJV

Lucifer refused to change his heart and acknowledge his wrongdoings. Instead, he became seated in his position. Today, he is still working out his retaliation against God by blinding the hearts of Christians. He is constant in his mission to cheat mankind of the earthly and eternal promises of God. The enemy is fully aware that he will never enjoy the glorious state of being in Heaven again, neither will he ever hear of his beauty and wonder. We can say that he is always offended at the righteous judgment of God, so much that he *"walks around like a roaring lion, seeking whom he may devour"* (1Pe 5:8 NKJV). He is not discriminating, so he uses anyone who is open and vulnerable.

Satan is devoted to his mission to *"steal, kill, and destroy"* man's life. He conspires with the kingdom of darkness to catch man off guard. The strategy is simple: study the nature and proclivities of man to know his strengths and weaknesses. Any place of strength in our lives is susceptible to extreme confidence and pride. This helps to build an inflated and false sense of self, which ultimately leads to failure. The areas of weakness in our person are typically entryways to the heart. John says that when Satan fell from Heaven, a third of the angels followed him (Rev 12:4). God ushered them into a realm of darkness (2Pe 2:4). This is a stark warning for Christians. The angels who joined Satan were open to the power of his influence.

"Therefore, submit to God. Resist the devil and he will flee from you."

~ James 4:7 NKJV

Offense Defined

offense
verb
offend | \ə-ˈfens\
offended; offending; offends

1. something that outrages the moral or physical senses
2. the act of displeasing or affronting; the state of being insulted or morally outraged
3. an infraction of law
4. a cause or occasion of sin[5]

The word offense is the term we have come to use for anything that is placed in our path having the potential to cause us to stumble. It's interesting that the Greek word *"skandalon,"* pronounced "skä'n-dä-lon," has a root meaning "any impediment placed in the way and causing one to stumble or fall; jump up or snap shut" in reference to the trigger of an animal trap.[6] For example, a hunter will set a trap designed for an animal to walk into it without noticing that it is there. A fisherman uses the same principle. He will cover a hook with bait to pull or entice the fish he would like to catch. When we experience an offense, our struggle is comparable to trapping a wild animal. All we know is that our focus has taken a turn and we are trapped in an endless pursuit of confusion and hurt. This unexplainable and annoying sensation is the reaction Satan needs to perform his best work against us.

Consider it this way: If you realize your plants are being eaten or your trash can is knocked over, then these are signs that you have uninvited wild animals on your property. The aim is not to kill, but to deter these pests from entering your property again, so you decide that you are going to set a snare. In this case, you would find a trapping

---

[5] https://www.merriam-webster.com/dictionary/offense
[6] G4625 –*skandalon*-Strong's Greek Lexicon (KJV)." Blue Letter Bible. Accessed 5 Sept, 2019., https://www.blueletterbible.org/lang/lexicon/lexicon.cfm?t=kjv&strongs=g4625

device large enough that most of the animal's body can fit in it before it reaches the trigger. When the trigger snaps closed the animal is caught and is able to move around. When hunting for sport and food, the serious hunter will entice a deer in the same sort of way, but the trap is different.

This time, the hunter must bed the trap in the hole he has dug and cover it up. At the opportune time, a deer will step right into the hole, getting caught in the trap. Initially, the injury is painful, and it tries its best to find a way out. Rather than examining the trap, the deer looks outward for its rescue. As the deer realizes his condition is dependent upon a source outside of itself, it begins to lose hope and gets used to the painful irritation of the trap. By the time the hunter discovers he has prey, the animal is so exhausted it does not have the strength to fight any longer. Hence, the hunter captures the animal and kills it later.

In a similar fashion, the initial offense creates questions that are designed to discourage or cause you to encircle the wrong done to you. You meditate on why or how the offense happened. Each time you share the offense openly, it is a cry to be heard, understood, and acquitted from the act and ensuing emotions. With each silent cry, the monument of confusion and pain is enlarged. Because the substance of explanations is lacking, the one wounded begins to accept the trap as being his way of doing things. Hereafter, he lives in the trap of offense. Rather than learning how to be set free, he fights to protect the trap of unforgiveness, anger, abuse, and rage. In the same way the animal's freedom is attached to someone setting it free, his mental, physical and emotional freedom is linked to God and His Word.

It Happens

"For there must also be factions among you, that those who are approved may be recognized among you."

~ 1Corinthians 11:19 NKJV

We are all prone to the trap of offense. Jesus said, *"It is impossible that no offences should come, but woe to him through whom they do come!"* (Lk 17:1 NKJV). In a perfect religious world, some claim that they are never bothered by the actions of another. In denial, they boast of their strength, not willing to acknowledge their inner grief about what they really think or feel. Then there are others who admit they have removed themselves from people and activities because of what was said or done. When Jesus makes this statement, He is in discourse with the disciples about the Kingdom's standard of living with one another. He was taking the time to impart knowledge and wisdom to them concerning what they could expect and how it is divinely perceived.

First, Jesus was absolute when He said, *"It is impossible that no offenses will come"* (Lk 17:1 NKJV), meaning that they are a part of life, and in many instances unavoidable. Every offense is not intentional. Second, He warned the one who causes the offense. There are certainly times we can offend someone without knowing it, but I believe Jesus is dealing with the person who sets out to offend another. He is challenging the disciples' motives – their hearts. Here we see that God does not make a distinction between the one who has no intention to offend and the one who intends to offend. The outcome is the same. Jesus says, *"Woe to the one through whom they come!"* (Lk 17:1 NKJV). The use of the word woe is an indication of the seriousness assigned to the offender. Simply stated, there is a strong consequence that follows the offender. God is concerned about how we treat one another. In either instance, whether intentional or unintentional, the believer is responsible for his actions towards other people.

Paul relates it this way, *"If it is possible, as much as depends on you, live peaceably with all men"* (Ro 12:18 NKJV). If we focus on the *"as much as depends on you,"* it demands that we examine our will by the Word of God. Herein the hard questions arise: "Why do I have to give in?" "What did I do?" "If it's not my fault, why did I get this treatment?" "Why wasn't I included?" "Why am I always the one left out?" These inner questions are what we inevitably charge against God's sovereignty. He has the right, the authority, power, and wisdom to carry out His will in our lives. After all, God is in control and rules over all things (Ps 103:19). Neither Satan nor people have authority over God. At the conclusion of this endless deposition of thoughts, the innermost question remains unanswered: "What is lying within me that hinders me from being at peace with my neighbor?"

Waiting Trigger

> *"Will a bird fall into a snare on the earth, where there is no trap for it? Will a snare spring up from the earth if it has caught nothing at all?"*
>
> ~ Amos 3:5 NKJV

When the hunter aims to trap an animal, he has studied the animal's nature and how it behaves. He will watch what the animal likes to eat and how it responds to danger and pleasure. The hunter has become familiar with the animal's strengths and weaknesses. Having knowledge of this information strengthens the impact. Any sportsman can tell you that when an animal's habitat is noisy, the creature is quick to discern a sound that does not come from the pack. So, a good hunter must be quiet and observant. A deer or fox does not have the ability to grocery shop, so nature becomes its store. The hunter will drop something the animal likes to eat or leave a scent - luring the animal to the trap. At the point the hunter believes he has an advantage over the prey, he lays the trap. His catch is successful, based on the right timing and favorable circumstances.

The enemy strikes or ensnares at the opportune time to catch us off guard. This is important because we must be aware that the enemy does not want to fight. He is determined to make an offensive move into our territory. Here, he has sized us up and developed a strategy, and based on his knowledge of our ways, he moves in for the attack. He is literally walking in and taking what he wants from us. When it comes to offense, he is stealing our peace and destiny. Times of happiness can be looked at as times of comfort because of the subtle intoxication of presumed stillness. A symptom of being drunk is the inability to exercise mental or physical control. Happiness is associated with some type of action or happening, which provokes feelings of contentment. This type of triumph has the power to make us feel invincible.

It is common to relish that feeling, not wanting it to change. Rather than examine our surroundings, we become intoxicated by the feeling of success. We recognize the lion as king of the jungle because it is a ferocious predator. Unlike other wild animals, the lion is large and not very fast. It is known to be intimidating because it is patient and methodical in its attack. Remember Peter warned, *"Be sober, be vigilant; because your adversary the devil walks about like a roaring lion, seeking whom he may devour"* (1Pe 5:8 NKJV). Peter's advice is wisdom. The only way to practice diligence is to exercise sobriety. The idea is to be watchful, not leaving yourself vulnerable or open to attack.

Peter was apparently familiar with the lion's ability to outwit its prey. Based on his words, there is not room for us to drink the intoxicating potions of pride, high-mindedness, neglect, or ignorance. They will impair our judgment. Although the lion does not have the physical speed of his fellow jungle citizens, he outruns them in intelligence. It is relaxed as he chases its prey; it trails behind, saving energy for a sprint at the end. The lion is willing to endure to the end because its mental gauge is already set on the big finish! Unaware of the lion's strategy, the other animals give up as they assume it has given out. The lion does not look for an opponent that will fight back; he is looking for one who will give up. The power of the lion's throne is rooted in its ability to be mentally strong and aware. Thus, when we assume everything is going well with us, we leave our doors and windows open, not controlling the portals of entry.

"In idleness there is perpetual despair." ~ Thomas Carlyle

What is Offense?

There is a similar impact when we deal with despair. Feelings of despair are closely related to depression, causing one to hibernate or become passive. The lethargy of despair reduces the energy to think; therefore, we walk around with a sense of emptiness. This is a great recipe for defeat. The worst, however, is to be idle. As the old saying goes, *"An idle mind is the devil's workshop."* This has everything to do with one who lacks focus or direction. We become easy prey when we lay down our armor. A good soldier is aware of his surroundings; therefore, he is prudent to always dress appropriately. He will resist the lure of laziness and make the choice to protect his heart by carrying the shield of faith. We can have God's Word and fail to walk in wisdom, leaving ourselves open to the trickeries of the enemy. Whether we experience happiness, despair, or idleness - unaware, each can create excellent conditions for attack.

When the enemy has worked to bring about offense in our lives, we make comments such as, "I can't believe this happened. I thought we were friends." The whole idea of offense is dealing with the concept of discovering what is hidden in plain sight. God has given us *"the mind of Christ,"* but we forsake His thoughts when we operate with limited insight of what is soul and spirit (1Cor 2:16 NKJV). If we ask the Lord to think through our minds and give us a discerning spirit, we will not be taken off guard when we are faced with an offense. The enemy is patient and is looking for the right time to attack each of us. No one is immune to being offended. No longer can we allow our vision to be inhibited by issues of our hearts.

"A hit dog will holler." ~ *19th Century Proverb*

Being raised in the rural South afforded me opportunities to hear stories that only made sense to the locals. I remember spending a Sunday evening with my grandparents and my grandfather suggested, "If you throw a rock at a pack of dogs, then the one that hollers is the one that got hit." I did not understand where he was going with his words of wisdom, but later in life those words resonated like a ringing bell. I can recall being in a meeting when the atmosphere abruptly shifted. The leader began to passionately filibuster in defense of his position. As the speech continued, I tried to remain focused, all the while remembering my grandfather's aphorism about the hollering dog. I kept my thoughts to myself as it was clear the leader was deeply offended by the words and actions of a select few people.

In this circumstance, the leader was the dog that got hit. Thayer's Greek Lexicon defines offense as, "the movable stick or trigger of a trap; any impediment placed in the way and causing one to stumble or fall."[7] It is important that we analyze the trigger and impediment. For a gun to fire, the trigger must be pressed for the bullet to be released. The trigger literally releases what has been concealed. For offense to occur, something has been lying dormant, hidden within the soul, long before the trigger was activated. Whatever has been lying there has a significant amount of power attached to it. It is the thing that successfully hinders your thoughts, feelings and behavior.

It can be said that the thing which is hidden can impede your walk. Jesus said, *"things that cause people to stumble are bound to come..."* (Lk 17:1 NIV). Have you ever been in a conversation with three or four people and one person left being offended? Later, after being questioned, the offended party was surprised that he was the only one bothered? For the others at the table, nothing was said or done that triggered the hidden issue. Having a healthy sense of self helps to alleviate the trauma of being offended, but it does not end there.

Testimony

As a teenager, I was well known in my rural high school and community. On occasion, I can remember being around certain people who seemed to have an issue with my presence. Sometimes I

---

[7] "G4625 - *skandalon* - Strong's Greek Lexicon (KJV)." Blue Letter Bible. Accessed 6 Sep, 2019. https://www.blueletterbible.org//lang/lexicon/lexicon.cfm?Strongs=g4625&t=kjv

found myself retreating to silence and wiping away tears of hurt because I was the punchline of a joke, or the roundtable discussion. Outwardly, I chose to cover my inward pain with a smile and a chuckle. It was very important to refrain from allowing my persecutors to see my hurt. I never really understood the reason I wasn't accepted by those people; the sting of their comments stained my heart with a sense of inferiority. Have you ever felt like you didn't measure up because someone negatively pointed out your inadequacies before others?

I was offended. My feelings were hurt, and my sense of worth was challenged. The truth is that I felt a strong insult and it needed to be resolved. I was insulted because of being mistreated without due cause. I was upset that certain people laughed openly at what was said, then privately they would criticize my persecutors. I was left feeling like a misfit. What started as offense led to approval seeking. Throughout my adolescent and college years, I walked the line of confusion. I was a Christian, loved Jesus, yet I wanted to experience the life everyone else enjoyed. I would practice cursing so I could be included in some conversations. I knew some of my behaviors were not representative of my faith in God, but it didn't stop me.

All the negative choices I made were a thin veneer, covering emotional pains and stigmas connected to growing up. This is all quite amusing because it was not until I was an adult that I realized the foundation of my ungodly behaviors were rooted in offense. When we are offended, we are inclined to feel shame, embarrassment, and anger. These negative emotions can lead to even more negative behavior, tailor-made to destroy the purposes and promises of God for our lives.

The act of being offended takes various forms and is distinguished by inward thoughts and emotions of unjust violation. What may have begun as a simple oversight or misunderstanding has evolved into a volcanic mountain, waiting to erupt. We commonly think of an offense from the standpoint of what someone has done to us. Rarely do we investigate whether the offense was intentional or not. Instead, we rely on the position that it should never have happened at all. The root of my offense was a seed of pride. I had to learn my acceptance was initiated and affirmed in God. I wasted good energy creating a persona that didn't even belong to me. I had offended the Lord and myself.

Ask yourself:

1. Explain why it's important to know why Lucifer was removed from Heaven.
2. Identify and describe how pride affects my life.
3. How do I apply, *"If it is possible, as much as lieth in you, live peaceably with all men?"*

Pray

Father, I am grateful for my salvation. Help me to recognize how often I have overlooked the very things I should pay attention to. I desire to take responsibility for how I feel and not place blame on others. Help me to be mindful of Jesus and His sacrifice for me. In Jesus' name. Amen.

Chapter 2
Garden Offense

"You ran well. Who hindered you from obeying the truth? This persuasion does not come from Him who calls you."
~ Galatians 5:7-8 NKJV

Everything God created was good; made to perfection with the goal of gaining pleasure through its reflection of Him. God, in His infinite wisdom and matchless creativity, formed the earth, the galaxies, the seasons and everything living, with His glorious excellence. The universe was fitted with everything that made it complete. It was here that the enemy planted the seed of sin, which has flourished in the earth. The resilience of the enemy's seed has successfully challenged the splendor of God's masterpiece. That seed took root and continues to flourish through every season. Although the fruit of Satan's trees are evil, they have eternal value in God's divine ecosystem. Ironically, God uses the contaminated fruit to carry out His will.

Scripture reveals that God is love and everything He created is good. To Isaiah God says, *"I form the light and create darkness, I make peace and create calamity; I, the Lord, do all these things"* (Is 45:7 NKJV). Here, the Lord is making it clear that He creates all things to work out the counsel of His will on earth. The opposing forces of light and darkness are necessary to cultivate truth in the garden of life. The loving nature of the Lord works in harmony with all of creation to manifest His divine will. Satan's influence is a complementary element to bring about God's redemptive plans.

Prior to Genesis, God knew mankind would sin and He already had a remedy for it. This is a key component to understanding and accepting the prospect that purpose is wrapped in circumstances and situations of life. The writer of Romans makes a declaration, *"And we know that all things work together for good to them that love God, to them who are the called according to His purpose"* (Ro 8:28 NKJV). The substance of this statement is overwhelming, yet an undeniable reality to embrace. We are accustomed to viewing life's happenings through the lens of carnality; therefore, we look to find justifiable reasons. The inability to adequately explain why something has occurred provokes a sense of inadequacy, which contributes to overwhelming the psyche and emotions. From this single line of carefully crafted words, there is an enduring truth revealed through the process: Accept that God is either allowing it or ordering it. Period.

There is so much we can take away from the happenings in the Garden of Eden. First, we must be on guard to listen and take heed to God's Word. Second, it's better to enlist the support of our Father when we are unsure of what we are hearing. When we reflect on what is accepted as the initial act of sin, we recognize Satan's manipulation towards a woman who was not mature in her understanding of God and herself. The acknowledgement of who we are, considering who God is, directs us to make wiser decisions.

Just like Eve, believers today who don't have adequate knowledge and insight of Satan's schemes are more susceptible for the seed of offense to be planted. He is looking for any available vessel to complete his mission of offending God through man. He used a woman, a man, a serpent and fruit. Had Eve been properly advised of the truth would she have made the choice to willfully obey the voice of the enemy? The point here has to do with intent. Was her intention to disobey God or to obey Satan? Based on the conversation in the garden, there is nothing that indicates Eve meant to disobey God. Intention must always be factored into offense.

From Genesis to Revelation, Satan has been exercising his petty pain by twisting and manipulating the minds and hearts of mankind. This is to offend God and destroy destiny. Before the foundation began, he was basking in the majesty of Heaven and eternity. Not willing to accept responsibility for his actions, he continues to rebel against God by using mankind's ignorance and pride. This pettiness is the catalyst for many broken hearts.

The earliest account is found in Genesis 3, where Adam and Eve were caught in their sin. Adam was clearly upset that Eve was the cause of their problem. In his petty state, Adam defended himself by saying, *"The woman whom You gave to be with me…"* (Gen 3:12 NKJV). I find this scene to be amusing and devastating. The humorous part is Adam's immature and spineless reaction to his own willful disobedience. On the contrary, unbeknownst to Adam, his issue manifested as a spiritual disease that has contaminated the bloodline of mankind. The Apostle Paul explains, *"Therefore, just as through one man sin entered the world, and death through sin, and thus death spread to all men, because all sinned"* (Ro 5:12 NKJV). At this time, the law had not been given, but the propensity to sin was born. To live in the clutch of offense is to live in sin. Each of these early examples of offense paint a vivid picture for our edification.

God Offended

"And the Lord was sorry that He had made man on the earth, and He was grieved in His heart."

~ Genesis 6:6 NKJV

As previously discussed, offending others has been present since the beginning of time. We know Satan is steeped in jealousy, anger, and deceit because of his loss of position. Revelation says that he is the *"accuser of the brethren"* (Rev 12:10 NKJV). If he can lure you to his carefully constructed trap, then he can use you against God. His petty accusations are not for God to deny you, but for you to deny the Lord. His bitterness runs deeply enough to orchestrate strategies to control your thoughts and emotions against God's Word. Satan knows that if his tactics are successful, then you will eventually go against the Lord. A heart infiltrated with an offense is inwardly focused on how to avenge itself at the expense of another. If you are honest with yourself, you will admit that you have experienced this before. Any time you can recall that you chose to obey your emotions, what others expect of you, or logic, then you have operated against the will of God and agreed with the adversary.

The Scripture describes Lucifer as the most highly decorated angel in Heaven until he began to equate or compete with God. His reckless state of rebellion led to his demise: his removal from Heaven forever. *"How you are fallen from heaven, O Lucifer, son of the morning! How you are cut down to the ground, you who weakened the nations!"* (Is 14:12 NKJV). This eviction was irreversible. He could no longer live in peace, worshipping the Lord in Heaven. The dormant issues of Lucifer's heart were awakened by his prideful and conceited attitude. He could not handle his position of leadership, beauty, talent and popularity. Offending God, Lucifer chose to stay on the path of rebellion.

When the Lord made mankind, He desired that we would be a source of pleasure for Him and it has never changed. Think about this: Our God, our Creator, knows everything about us and desires to find pleasure in every part of our lives. The Old Testament prophet says, *"The Lord your God in your midst, the Mighty One, will save; He will rejoice over you with gladness, He will quiet you with His love, He will rejoice over you with singing."* (Ze 3:17 NKJV). He is like a proud daddy looking at his babies, beaming with joy at the sight of His children. His creation reflects His own glory. In the garden, the glory of God's original plan was manifested as peace, blessings, and prosperity. It was through the sin of disobedience that shame, loss, sickness, and death were launched in the earth.

> *"The LORD takes pleasure in those who fear Him, in those who hope in His mercy."*
>
> ~ Psalm 147:11 NKJV

God's desire is for all living creatures to have an intimate knowledge of Him. This means that by design and purpose, every creature should have a first-hand, personal understanding of the Lord, not based on someone else's words. *"For thus says the Lord, Who created the heavens, Who is God, Who formed the earth and made it, Who has established it, Who did not create it in vain, Who formed it to be inhabited: 'I am the Lord, and there is no other'"* (Is 45:18 NKJV). When Moses was receiving his assignment to release the children of Israel from Egyptian slavery, he asked the Lord how to answer questions when asked about the God who sent him. This was vital since the Egyptians worshipped various gods and he knew the Israelites would want to know which god had sent him. God told Moses, tell them *"I AM that I AM" sent you* (Ex 3:14 NKJV). Although they had been enslaved for 430 years, they knew Jehovah, the all-powerful, all-wise, all-knowing and living God, the eternal God. Habakkuk declares that the creation's knowledge of God is to extend beyond the land to all the seas. This is everything, everybody and everywhere. The Lord's overarching delight is that we – His creation – would delight in Him.

    Reading the Bible, we know offense is not unfamiliar to the Lord. God has been repeatedly offended, beginning in Genesis. Think about it. Cain and Abel inherited the inclination to sin from their parents. This inheritance spread like a disease, infecting every individual born. Not only did the disease spread, it became so toxic that after Cain's murder of his brother, God decided to destroy mankind. The Creator was offended at the willful state of wickedness of His creation. The world was consumed with hatred and its ensuing violence and murder. *"So, the Lord said, 'I will destroy man whom I have created from the face of the earth, both man and beast, creeping things and birds of the air, for I am sorry that I have made them'"* (Gen 6:7 NKJV). We must be clear in understanding the righteous judgment of God. His offense in man's behavior led Him to destroy almost all of mankind. Today, we stand as recipients of His great mercy and grace, *"But Noah found grace in the eyes of the Lord"* (Gen 6:8 NKJV). Daily, we awaken to the wonder of His mercy, providing another chance to "get it right". Though offended, the never-ending and unfailing love of God compelled Him to save - cover and redeem!

"Our society strives to avoid any possibility of offending anyone – except God."
~ Rev. Billy Graham

Nothing has changed. God is still offended when we sin. In case you are thinking, "If God can be offended, so can I." Stop it. While this reasoning may seem justifiable, it is unbiblical. God's offense has to do with His image being reflected in man. God is holy. When we sin, the act offends the holy character of the Lord. *"For God did not call us to uncleanness, but in holiness"* (1Thess 4:7 NKJV). We are called to live a holy life because God commands that our lifestyles bring glory and honor to His name. It's in Christ's sacrifice, that the penalty for our sin is satisfied. Paul tells the Romans, *"Much more then, having now been justified by His blood, we shall be saved from wrath through Him. For when we were enemies we were reconciled to God through the death of His Son, much more, having been reconciled, we shall be saved by His life"* (Ro 5:9-10 NKJV). God chose Jesus' life as an example to us that we can live without being bound to sin. His death paid the price to set us free from sin's bondage. *"For even the Son of Man did not come to be served, but to serve, and to give His life a ransom for many"* (Mk 10:45 NKJV). Jesus took our place! *"For He made Him who knew no sin to be sin for us, that we might become the righteousness of God in Him"* (2Cor 5:21 NKJV). It is noteworthy that sin is so heinous, that God chose to sacrifice Jesus so that we can live. In this sense, God's righteousness demands that He is offended at our sin.

Ask yourself:

1. In what way does my life bring pleasure to God?
2. List and describe the areas of sin I justify and reason within myself.
3. Describe the difference it makes in how I feel about offending someone I know and someone who is a stranger to me.

Pray

Father, I give you everything within me that is contrary to Your will. I take every impure motive and thought, and I cast them at the foot of the cross. I submit my mind to Your Word and command it to agree. Search me, Oh God, and show me what is hidden that I have overlooked in my life. I commit myself to You and Your will. In Jesus' name. Amen.

Part Two
The
POSITION

A place where someone or something
is located or has been put;
a particular way in which someone or
something is placed or arranged.

~ Oxford Dictionary

What is your Position?

"I will stand my watch and set myself on the rampart and watch to see what He will say to me, and what I will answer when I am corrected."

~ Habakkuk 2:1 NKJV

It has been determined that we will experience occasions to be offended by a word, action or behavior. This event has the power to affect you negatively, but it is temporary in duration. A person with a temporary reaction can be very different than the one who exhibits a need or desire to remain in a position, not prescribed by God for long periods of time. The one who processes through an event, weighing the situation from all angles, likely chooses to respond in a mature manner. On the contrary, the person who reacts quickly and emotionally, rarely has given much thought about negative consequences. The reactionary choice is often connected to unresolved negative events of the past. The refusal or failure to respond can be considered an oppression, or demonic influence that hinders your healing or deliverance.

Bible scholars typically agree that believers can't be possessed by a demon but agree that the likelihood of being oppressed by a demon is possible. For me, I find it to be a simple conclusion that reflects Scriptural truths. From Genesis to Revelation, we see the common thread wherein the enemy looks to *"steal, kill and destroy."* His assignment is in direct opposition to the assignment of Jesus, to *"come and give you life more abundantly."* Some Christians have difficulty with the concept of being oppressed by a spirit because the Bible never labels offense as being a spirit. In order to bring clarity to the picture, I make a distinction between an offense and the Spirit of Offense. An offense is a single event or occurrence. The Spirit of Offense is a state or position one has assumed as a consequence of having been offended.

Chapter 3
Anatomy of Offense

"He who loves his brother abides in the light, and there is no cause for stumbling in him."

~ 1 John 2:10 NKJV

When our daughter was in undergrad, she opted to take anatomy at the local technical college during summer break. When I asked why she chose anatomy, she suggested she needed to be able to study it "like she needs to" and that it was "way too much" with a semester's load of classes. When offended, it is reasonable to explore or perform an autopsy of the situation. It requires a diligent look at all the factors involved; the who, what, when and why. What makes the anatomy class important is that practitioners must master the parts of the body and how each component works in conjunction with the cells, organs and tissues. Sometimes an autopsy is performed when a person dies, and the cause of death is questionable. In the same way, when an offense occurs it can leave us wondering what happened and why it affects you the way it does.

I propose that there are three primary characters under examination as they relate to offense: The Offender; The Offended; and the Unoffended.

The Offender

"But whoever causes one of these little ones who believe in Me to sin, it would be better for him if a millstone were hung around his neck, and he were drowned in the depth of the sea."
~ Matthew 18:6 NKJV

By definition, the word "offender" is a legal term. In a courtroom, the one who breaks the law, or commits the crime is considered to be the offender. Based on the law, the violation is deemed to be punishable by a fine or imprisonment. The laws of the land have determined what is lawful and what isn't. As citizens, we are to obey the laws because they are designed to protect against the wrongful behavior of others.

As previously mentioned, Jesus advised that there is always an opportunity for offense among those in a community. His counsel brings clarity to the inherent nature of relationships. All spheres of today's age are saturated with people who offend for the sake of their image, reputation, and religious beliefs. People will disagree and fall out with one another, often for no apparent reason, other than difference of opinion, attitude, thoughts and intentions. When the guilty party, the offender, has been identified it is imperative to determine whether the offense was intentional or unintentional.

When one is named as the offender, that person has said or done something that hurt another. Whether intentional or not, the one offended experiences a degree of hurt. If it isn't a person's motive to offend someone, he typically is convicted and seeks forgiveness for the purpose of reconciliation. On the contrary, the one who is determined to offend another won't display any sense of conviction because his objective is fulfilled. He feels a sense of justifiable vengeance. In either case, the seriousness of Jesus' caution is understood by His use of the word "woe." In Scripture, "woe" is a literal expression related to the expectation of God's judgment. This type of judgment is associated with intense grief, regret, anger or sorrow.

This crucial element gives us insight into how the Lord regards and assesses our relationships with other people.

The Offended

"If you are reproached for the name of Christ, blessed are you, for the Spirit of glory and of God rests upon you. On their part He is blasphemed, but on your part, He is glorified."

~ 1Peter 4:14 NKJV

The offended is acknowledged as the one who is hurt by the words or actions of another. It is characteristic that the offended will change his perspective of the offender, other people, and circumstances based on how he regards or thinks about the offense. On the surface, this is a justifiable reaction. After all, no one deserves the discouragement, disrespect, disgrace, or disregard that accompanies offense. The person who has accepted an offense has literally agreed to its power over his life.

I compare this to a person who has decided to take a sleeping pill before going to work. The medication is a sedative, which is designed to make you relax. This can produce great loss. The one who has taken offense has theoretically taken the pill. No longer is he alert and focused, he is now unable to pay attention to significant details. Sometimes the offended is unable to discern the difference in soul and spiritual responses. This is key because he rarely sees his potential to hurt himself and others. The offended must never forget that the enemy's motive is to *"steal, kill and destroy,"* so it is a much easier task if he can convince us to partner with him in working against ourselves.

The Proverbs writer says, *"The discretion of a man makes him slow to anger, and his glory is to overlook a transgression"* (Prov 19:11 NKJV). In the Hebrew, *"abar"* (5674), means "to pass over, or by."[8] This verse suggests that it isn't wise to react impulsively to offense, but we should look for a way to let it go. The greatest challenge comes in knowing how to respond to the offense.

The Unoffended

"Also, do not take to heart everything people say, lest you hear your servant cursing you."

~ Ecclesiastes 7:21-22 NKJV

The most uncommon and powerful character of all, is the one who is not inclined to be offended. Although everybody will experience offense at some point, this is the person who chooses not to give in to it. He stands in his truth concerning self. The writer of Ecclesiastes relates this person to one who considers his personal imperfections as cause to give others room to be imperfect also. He is not swayed by what others think, feel or believe as he is confident that their words or behavior has no bearing on his character, reputation, or well-being. This steadiness flows from the place of inner peace, humility and honesty. Often this person walks in a grace forged by the flames of his environment, past hurts, or faith. This person has decided how much energy and attention will be devoted to dealing with someone else's issue.

The attitude of the unoffended is uncommon. This unique and powerful person has the ability to influence positive change for Christ. Keep in mind that Jesus had many opportunities to be offended, but he chose not to be. He remained focused on his assignment. Unlike us, he could hear the thoughts of people's hearts. He knew when people questioned his identity and purpose, yet he refused to accept the offensive actions. If Jesus had gotten emotionally

---

[8] "H5674 - `abar - Strong's Hebrew Lexicon (KJV)." Blue Letter Bible. Accessed 5 Sep, 2019. https://www.blueletterbible.org//lang/lexicon/lexicon.cfm?Strongs=h5674&t=kjv

caught up in what was happening around him, he would have stepped out of character. His strategy was epic! When questioned he was known to answer certain questions with a question. People choose whether to be offended or not. Every believer has the power and authority to refuse offense. The victor is the one who does not bow to the incident.

> *"Great peace have those who love Your law, and nothing causes them to stumble."*
>
> ~ Psalm 119:165 NKJV

Cause of Offense

> *"For consider Him who endured such hostility from sinners against Himself, lest you become weary and discouraged in your souls."*
>
> ~ Hebrews 12:3 NKJV

It is of grave importance that we discover the root cause of why we become offended. To deal with offense means there is a "cause and effect" relationship. Becoming offended is the effect or result of some event that has occurred. This is an interesting concept because it requires us to investigate or inquire why the offense happened. Without something lying dormant in our psyche, there wouldn't be any influence to provoke pain, disappointment or misunderstanding. Think about it. For something to bother you to the point you react, it carries some type of preconceived weight in your life. Meaning, the issue was already there.

Each time Satan tries to use offense as a method to throw us off course and sin, he has learned what is lying dormant within our lives. He is not all-knowing, but he is diligent. Satan and his helpers study our lives from the time we are born. They examine the family structure we are connected to and its patterns. Once we are born, they have cleverly designed methods to attack us without our knowledge.

When we fail to adequately handle events, which have caused disappointment and pain, Satan uses them as opportunities to set traps.

There are times we do not pay attention to what has happened in our being. For example, many will take a stance of being very unresponsive to the negative issues of life. If you were taught to ignore the insults and ignorance of others, then you may have an underlying issue with confrontation. It is not always something that occurs with another individual but is often an unresolved issue with self. In reality, we can be offended and live years pretending that something did not bother us. Typically, if we respond indifferently it is a sign we were bothered. When we are indifferent, we are showing attitudes of apathy or displaying a lack of concern. While we aren't to be controlled by the words and actions of others, it is healthy to take negatives to the foot of the cross.

We should examine why we make comments like, "It doesn't matter." "I don't care what they do, what does it have to do with me?" Most of these remarks are an invisible shield of protection. This shield works to convince you that diverting a conversation or denying someone exists, will make the pain of offense go away. In particular, if you've been prone to hurt feelings and you decide you are no longer allowing anyone to bother you, acting as if it doesn't bother you is not the cure. The cure is found in self-appraisal, or self-awareness. When we allow the inner assessment, we essentially permit the Lord to enter and examine our souls; He lets us know what is there.

If we do this without God, we are unable to objectively assess the changes that need to be made. Some awareness takes us on a journey. We are challenged to discover the self the public sees and the private self. By asking the Lord to examine the inner person, we have a more accurate view of what is happening. If we look at the word "offend," the meaning is connected to something that causes you to stumble. It isn't the actions of another, but more so how you choose to surrender your thoughts about what has been said or done. The more intimate we walk with the Lord the less inclined we should be to stumble. Paul said it best, *"Examine yourselves to see whether you are in the faith; test yourselves"* (2 Cor 13:5 NIV).

Purpose of Offense

"The thief does not come except to steal, and to kill, and to destroy."

~ John 10:10 NKJV

It is possible to live a long, successful life without ever knowing your purpose. Imagine standing before the Judgment Seat of Christ and your life is being examined by the book that God wrote about you before you were born. As you are questioned about why your divine accomplishments were not fulfilled, you suddenly realize that blaming the enemy is useless. He lived to *"steal, kill and destroy"* anyone and anything belonging to God. When he chooses the weapon of offense, it has the power to disrupt and ultimately destroy your marriage, family, health, finances, friendships, career, and ministry. Although Satan is strong, in Christ, you have the power to overcome him.

Offense challenges unity and effectiveness. Unity in the Body of Christ glorifies God. Before the cross, Jesus interceded for the church to be united in the same way that He was united in God. Specifically He prayed, *"That they all may be one, as You, Father, are in Me, and I in You; that they also may be one in Us, that the world may believe that You sent Me"* (John 17:21 NKJV). We must be constantly reminded that Jesus came to earth with the purpose that through His sacrifice, the world would be saved. His demonstration was perfected at the cross and through the resurrection. If we allow division to permeate the community of Christian believers, we have lost our sacrifice on earth. Dying to self is a daily discipline for the believer.

The world already knows how to come together for a common purpose, but they don't know how to unite in true love. What the enemy offers is counterfeit, so we must be conscientious to live what we confess. The Apostle Paul instructs, *"We give no offense in anything, that our ministry may not be blamed"* (2Cor 6:3 NKJV). The focus is always that the lost would come into a right relationship with the Lord. There are over 70 references to offense in the Bible. This is a strong clue that the subject of offense demands our attention. As believers, whatever we do is to be done in the spirit of Christ. Whenever the church unites in God, we will see the greatest revival on earth!

By definition and design, offense is orchestrated to trap, or hinder a person from progressing. This progression is directly attached to your God-ordained power and purpose. As believers, we must remain sober in our understanding of spiritual warfare. If we are living for Jesus, we will be challenged to submit our entire being over to him. Satan is clear that he has a limited time on earth, but we aren't always conscious of his tricks. He manipulates us to follow our flesh, or soulish desires. Satan is fully aware of his limitations and he also understands the soul of man. He is secure in knowing he is unable to steal our salvation, and equally confident in his abilities to wreak havoc and frustration on us. His strategies are developed by listening and observing each person's threshold for emotional endurance. He is partially satisfied when we reach the point of questioning our faith in God, or our identity in Him. He understands the importance of image. Remember God said, *"Let's make man in Our image, according to Our likeness…"* (Gen 1:26 NKJV). Satan will not stop in his quest to destroy the image of God in our lives. It is important to recognize that the picture of who we are is reflected in our character, not our reputation. My dad taught, "Your character is who you really are, deep down on the inside." The Lord regards true character – not appearance. When Satan's influence becomes so powerful that he can sway us to behave in unrighteous ways, he has gained a foothold.

The world buys into imagery, or what looks desirable. Keep in mind that offense began in the garden when Satan lured Eve to go after what appealed to her appetite. Hundreds of years later, after the Exodus, Moses went up on Mt. Sinai for about six weeks. For three months, it was Moses who delivered them from Pharaoh, led them safely through the wilderness, made sure they were fed and had water to drink. Because of the loving concern he had for them, you would think the Israelites would have been secure and mature enough to carry-on as if Moses were present. After all, he did not leave them alone, he left Aaron and Hur to watch over them in his absence. Since Moses did not come down from the mountain when they thought he should have, they became impatient and feared that he would not return. In their frustration, they looked to Aaron to supply a replacement for Moses; they wanted something or someone else to look up to (Ex 32). They wanted another image to follow.

Then and now, we are drawn towards people who appeal to the images we wish to be associated with. Therefore, by Satan's design, he loves it when the image of the Godly family is destroyed, when marriages are estranged, churches divided, and fellow believers are enemies; then our witness to the world has very little effect. Why? The witness of the church diminishes when there isn't a distinction between the unbeliever and the believer. We have been called to show love despite how we feel. *"This is my commandment, that you love one another as I have loved you"* (John 15:12 NKJV). This is the type of love that compels us to be and do what we must for the sake of the cross. Keep in mind that every believer has a cross he must carry. When we are abused, hurt, deceived, betrayed and offended, we are identifying with Christ. Satan is an enemy of God and he worked against Jesus; he works against us also. Meditate on Paul's words: *"…that I may know him and the power of his resurrection, and may share his sufferings, becoming like him in his death"* (Phil 3:10 ESV). To know the Lord also means to know the pain of offense. I believe Satan's agenda is division, his tool is offense, and his goal is destruction.

Effect of Offense

> *"For we do not have a High Priest who cannot sympathize with our weaknesses, but was in all points tempted as we are, yet without sin."*
>
> ~ Hebrews 4:15 NKJV

Being offended, has the power to affect us personally and interpersonally. Many people report the impact of offense as provoking emotional responses that they sometimes struggle with resolving. There are people who deny being offended by the actions of others, but live in a cauldron of anger and resentment connected to an incident or event with another party. Without question, the person who chooses to be offended has opened the door to a variety of emotions that have the potential to lead to devastating choices.

Before going further, let us take a look at the difference in feelings and emotions. If you were asked to give a definition for feelings, what would you say? Can you describe what feelings are without the use of the word emotion? When asked to define what feelings meant without using the word emotions, here are some insightful perspectives:

"A behavior of the mind that causes a person to have unconscious bias towards a specific action directed at themselves or others that elicits a response either positive or negative."

~ Terri Ryant Bennett
Housewife

"Feelings are a reaction or response based upon what a person believes, understanding that their beliefs are usually formed based upon past experiences. Peace comes to mind. At one time in my life chaos was everywhere – job and home. I discovered I could have peace if I began to change my thoughts."

~ Mary Young
Pastor and Entrepreneur

"Feelings…how your heart reacts to what your brain thinks"

~ Cindy Gilreath
Nurse

"Arousal of thoughts that evoke body and mind sensations that may or may not require an action."

~ Dr. Yvonne Commodore
Professional Educator and Minister

"It is a state of mind deriving from one's circumstances to believe with firm certainty the innermost part of something or someone."

~ Andrena King, M.Ed.
Career Coach

"Internalized intuitions involving the heart."

~ Joseph W. Ward
Senior National Sales Director

"Feelings are the catalyst for movement derived from the inner soul and spirit."

~ Gail Glover Faust
Author, Professional Dancer, Life Coach and Minister

    I suggest that we are so familiar with our feelings, that we do not recognize how they are related to our words and behaviors. Feelings and emotions have been given to us by our Creator. It is difficult to understand how to explain the death of a parent if there are no feelings and emotions attached to it. Giving birth to our children brought feelings of great joy and pain. Would you have ever recognized the true love of a mate, if your love was absent of feelings and emotions? What lessons would you learn if your failures were never met with sadness and disappointment? We must pause to identify our emotions and ask the question: "Why?" There is some thought that guides an emotional response. So, our thoughts – feelings - tend to guide our emotions. These thoughts are learned and are often tied to our past experiences. Emotions can mask our true feelings, but beneath the emotion is the truth. Our feelings are purposed to bring understanding in our lives. Without emotions and feelings, our lives would be stale and empty. I believe it's safe to say that our emotions have the power to dictate our future victories, struggles and failures.

> *"I've learned that people will forget what you said, people will forget what you did, but people will never forget how you made them feel."*
> ~ Maya Angelou

The Bible clearly describes our Creator as having emotions. God is scripted as experiencing anger, love, hate, compassion, grief, and joy in terms that associate His ways with humanity. I find it fascinating that the Lord can relate to His creation in this way. We can say that God understands our emotions and feelings. This expressive association is called anthropomorphism. We were created *"in the image and likeness"* of God. The Apostle Paul speaks of Jesus Christ as *"the image of the invisible God, the firstborn of all creation"* (Col 1:15 NKJV). This essentially suggests that we can examine Jesus' life and know the humanity of our Creator. The Hebrew word *"tselem,"* (tseh'·lem), means an outline or representation of the original.[9] This word points to the function of the original, rather than the

---

[9] Jeff A. Benner, Ancient Hebrew Research Center, "The Image of God", https://www.ancient-hebrew.org/god-yhwh/the-image-of-god.htm

representative. In other words, we can see God's attributes at work in His Son. So, I believe man was created with a conscious, moral and intelligent nature like God. Herein our emotions and feelings are merely an imitation of God's emotions and feelings. Scripture confirms this, *"For we do not have a High Priest who cannot sympathize with our weaknesses, but was in all points tempted as we are, yet without sin"* (Heb 4:15 NKJV). This is key to our understanding that we were meant to be emotional creatures. The intent was for man to share God's feelings and emotions. The problem is that man is a poor steward over them. Unlike man, God's emotional expressions are forged in righteousness rather than sin. If the mind is renewed to the truth of God's Word, our emotions will follow suit. It is critical that we examine what we think about our life experiences. We must ask ourselves if our thoughts about people and events line up with God's Word.

Our emotions are merely an indicator, not a guide for living. Sometimes our emotions get out of hand and we allow ourselves to become servants to how we feel. If someone makes us angry, we can allow the feeling to linger in our minds long enough that we react in malicious and reckless ways. Be aware that the anger is secondary to emotions like fear, fatigue, or embarrassment. This, however, is not how God's emotions are displayed. For the believer, being angry to the point of seeking revenge is beyond the boundaries of righteousness. Our emotions hinge on the opportunity to sin. The Holy Spirit doesn't lead us to sin, neither does He condone it. This is certainly not God's way. We ought to be constantly reminded of our power to choose the Lord's Way over our own.

EMOTIONS	**FEELINGS**
Produced in the Body	Produced in the Mind
Emotions are physical states that arise as a response to external stimuli	Feelings are mental associations and reactions to emotions
Aroused before feelings	Caused by emotions

Physical states	Mental associations and reactions
Can be observed through the physical	Can be hidden reaction

God is no stranger to offense. At first glance, it appears we can associate the anger of God with revenge, but it is quite the opposite. Before the flood, God became deeply offended at the overwhelming sin on the earth. People were out of control (Gen 6:5). They had become violent and were worshiping idols, even one another. Women were having children with fallen angels (Jude 6-7). This behavior was prohibited as it was a clear indication of the disregard of God's natural order in reproduction. Angels were not to marry (Matt 22:30). In the Lord's feeling of offense, He displayed anger because of his sorrow. *"And the LORD was sorry that He had made man on the earth, and He was grieved in His heart"* (Ge 6:6 NKJV). The Hebrew translation colors His regret as a pain so great it "fabricated or carved" His heart. When we are offended the impact has the power to change our hearts, or how we feel.

Unlike man, God's feelings and emotions are always consistent with His holy and righteous character. Despite God's intense grief, He continued to allow man to live and thrive. His feelings did not override his ultimate plan. The Scripture also notes Jesus as experiencing the same feelings and emotions that we do. He demonstrated anger towards the Pharisees (John 11:33, 38), sadness as he entered Jerusalem (Lk 19:41), hope as he endured abuse (Heb 12:2), joy as the gospel was preached (Lk 10:21), faith in God (John 15:12), and love for mankind (John 11:5; Mk 10:21). So, we can see that feelings and emotions are not bad. We must follow Jesus' example in stewarding over our emotions in a holy and healthy manner. When the emotions are not disciplined by the rule of righteousness, we enter sin.

As mentioned earlier, the church is a community of believers. We are the ones who have been called out of darkness into marvelous light. What is so marvelous about a dark light? We are not to live as the world in how we deal with one another. The church is to be a place wherein we unite to bring glory and honor to the Lord. Unfortunately, there is grave danger in avoidance or failure to acknowledge and confront offense in the church. When avoiding issues becomes the norm, it produces vulnerability. Ironically, what should be confronted and opposed has become empowered when offenses aren't dealt with. Therefore, the strength of the organization is compromised. Often there is an offensive tone between members and leaders. Today, even the mouth of the prophet is often known to prophesy offensively. Paul wrote, *"But he who prophesies speaks edification and exhortation and comfort to men"* (1Cor 14:3 NKJV).

According to God, it does matter the way we handle one another. There should not be any reason that we fail to exercise grace in our dealings. When offenses are confronted, they are the best opportunities to model Christian behavior in conflict resolution. The Apostle Paul advocates that unity is preserved when the body operates in humility, gentleness, patience and love for one another (Eph 4:2-4). These Christian virtues are the key to establishing a healthy atmosphere amongst believers. No one likes to be confronted when they are out of order, but the way in which you choose to handle them can make the worst situations bearable. When operating within a community of faith, no one is perfect, but all should have the standard of God's Word to govern their dealings. In other words, we are to imitate the Savior's ways. As leaders of the church, we are to adequately prepare the saints in how to conduct ministry and build one another up, in so doing we are maturing in unity and faith (Eph 4:13).

EGO

"Do you see a man wise in his own eyes? There is more hope for a fool than for him."

~ Proverbs 26:12 NKJV

When we are offended the effect is like rejection, so the first response is to defend self. Why? The need to defend and question points inward. This is the part of the conscious mind where esteem is housed. The problem comes in where the ego is out of balance. If we have a low sense of self-worth, we are apt to seek approval and acceptance from others. This deficit of self-worth is desperate to be filled from outside sources, instead of emanating from within. The need for outside validation makes offense an easy trap. Offense challenges your ego.

The ego is that invisible voice within that speaks of how one esteems or sees himself. Ego is one's sense of self-worth. Typically, people associate the ego as a negative, but I don't. Scripture teaches us to *"love your neighbor as yourself"* so we must have a healthy regard for who we are (Matt 22:39). The writer of Proverbs says, *"For as he thinks in his heart, so is he"* (Prov 23:7 NKJV). Thus, whatever you think of yourself is essentially what you will become. If you see yourself as being an achiever, you will achieve. If you see yourself as being valuable, you won't settle or accept anyone or anything that diminishes your worth.

It is interesting to note that Jesus relates this principle another way. He says, *"For from within, out of the heart of men, proceed evil thoughts"* (Mk 7:21 NKJV). Jesus is getting to the root reason. Our estimation of self is not found in the shallow waters of our accolades and achievements. Deep within, the heart is the fountain of our self-image and esteem.

> *"Few want to hear this, but it's true, and it can be enormously helpful in life: If you're constantly being hurt, offended, or angered, you should honestly evaluate your inflamed ego."*
> ~ Brant Hanson[10]

The person with an overinflated ego and the one with a low ego are both susceptible to offense. The overinflated ego is characterized

---

[10] https://www.goodreads.com/author/quotes/7360387.Brant_Hansen?page=1

as being prideful, arrogant and selfish. This emotional volcano is only concerned with self and no one else. This type of ego will take issue with the slightest incident and create a mountain. The one with a low ego, or low estimation of self is sensitive, and his feelings are attached to anything he perceives to be negative. On the surface, it appears this person is tender-hearted and unassuming, but he shares the self-consuming mind of the overinflated ego. In both cases, the issue of self is extreme.

The Bible doesn't command us to have high self-esteem, or self-worth. Why is this? Our worth or esteem is found in who we are in Christ. This fact levels the ground. I am certainly not implying that we are to have a low view of ourselves. Keep in mind that we are made in the image of God. Therefore, our worth is not dependent upon what we have accomplished, what we own, or the connections we have with others. The world upholds these qualities as a means of separating or qualifying people for acceptance or rejection. Consequently, the more a person feels respected and accepted by those of higher status, the better he feels about himself. This increases his self-esteem and inflates his ego. If you buy into this standard of measure for your life and it is taken away, then you have lost your self-esteem.

Whether we are accepted by the affluent, powerful or popular, none of that matters to the Lord. He wants us to know that our value is not limited to man's standards. Who we are and what we can become is beyond what we have the ability to conceive. *"Eye hath not seen, nor ear heard, neither have entered into the heart of man the things which God hath prepared for them that love Him"* (1Cor 2:9 NKJV). Let us see ourselves as God sees us: We are blessed, highly favored, and nothing is impossible for us because we believe God! For it is in Him that we live, move and have our very being.

Ask yourself:

1. When was the last time I felt offended?
2. Describe how my emotions have worked against me in the past.

3. Based on what I know about Jesus' teachings, explain what He taught about offense.

Pray

Father, I recognize that I have been offended and I am an offender. I don't want my feelings and emotions to rule my life any longer. Cleanse my heart and mind and help me to think on the things which are good, true, and of a good report concerning others. I commit myself to You and Your will. In Jesus' name. Amen.

Chapter 4
The Pathology of Offense

"Behold, you desire truth in the inward parts, and in the hidden part You will make me to know wisdom."

~ Psalm 51:6 NKJV

Nothing "just happens" in life. I remember the joy of being an aunt for the first time. I prided myself on always watching over my nephew and trying to be sure he was safe, happy and at peace. He was a calm and complacent child with a gentle and forgiving nature. Years later, prior to his entering college, I recognized life had altered his peace. Something had shifted. For the first time I detected that everything wasn't alright, and it was affecting his attitude and perspective. His behavior pointed to what seemed like an inward torment, but he wouldn't tell me what he was dealing with. The same thing happens when we come down with an illness that requires medical attention. The nurse or doctor will question us about symptoms, the time of onset, and the possible exposure. We are charged with answering honestly. If the clinician can accurately determine the pathology of the condition, then he is better able to diagnose and treat the problem. My nephew wouldn't talk, so I was at a loss because I didn't know if or how I could help him.

The science of pathology is based on the principles of "cause and effect." If you showed up in the emergency room with bruises over your body, you would be expected to explain what happened. Unless there was an accident, incident or disease, a healthy person would not have those symptoms. A careful physician would investigate the condition by ordering scans and blood work. Studying and comparing the findings enables the doctor to trace the root cause of the condition. The root serves as the basis, or source of treatment. If you choose to ignore the bruises, or if the doctor treats the bruises without knowing how they occurred, you could die. The advice of many medical professionals is that you are to become familiar with your body so that you know when something is not right, or normal.

When we are offended there is a tendency to direct our focus on the one we perceive is guilty of some hurtful action. Rarely have I spoken with anyone who is quick to admit the rooted reason they feel offended. In the same way when a seed is planted in good soil, it takes root and begins to grow, wrong beliefs or attitudes can be rooted within the heart if they are never examined. The rooted reason has a direct correlation to a past issue which was never dealt with sufficiently. Many deny that anything has happened, for some that may be true, but too often that is not the case.

The rooted reason may be a character weakness, lack of exposure to different views, the absence of counsel and accountability, or an injured soul. Most focus on being judged, criticized, misunderstood, rejected, or unfairly victimized. This skewed perception is a hindrance to really taking time to inventory the issues of the heart. We must acknowledge that all our life is experienced through our natural senses. We live in the present, and we have a memory bank that seems to record life's happenings in a system of short and long-term memory. Our memories are an efficient record-keeping arrangement that stores information based on how we have received it. For example, as a wife, if your engagement was an event showing that your fiancé was intentional to make it special, you will remember how you felt for the rest of your life. That memory may be inclusive of what you were wearing, the atmosphere of the room, who was there and perhaps the food. The same type of details would be recorded if your fiancé demonstrated little to no preparation for the engagement. One memory would be positive and the other would be negative. What is most interesting is that the brain has a way of retaining the information, which is most important to us, whether it is good or bad. Information travels from short-term to long-term memory based on its importance to us in terms of use and impact. Researchers believe our long-term memories don't have limitations; therefore, we are able to recall memories from as early as three or four years old.

Our emotions stem from our brain, or memory. When emotions aren't properly stewarded, thoughts begin to control emotions and decisions. This failure to effectively manage our thoughts can infect the heart, which affects the thinking. I relate this to having heart disease. The physical body is unable to live without a beating heart, but the body can function without certain other organs. For example, we can live without our spleen and women can live without their reproductive organs. No one can live without the heart. The heart is the organ that sends blood around the body, supplying oxygen and nutrients so that we can be healthy. It also removes harmful wastes. So, whatever is in the heart, it circulates through the body. When the heart is offended, the person is unable to think or reason without bias. Every situation is potentially judged or viewed through the diseased or offended heart.

> *"Keep your heart with all diligence, for out of it spring the issues of life."*
>
> ~ Proverbs 4:23 NKJV

In ancient civilizations, the heart was the motor, or organ, responsible for movement of the entire body. If the heart was strained it meant that the entire body felt it. If you trace each time the Scripture refers to the heart, you will find it emphasized over 1000 times. The Bible relates it as the center or core of our being, describing it as a physical organ and a hidden container for the intellect and emotions. The issues contained in our hearts have the power to influence our attitudes and decisions. Therefore, the Proverbs writer warns us to protect our hearts from being contaminated (Prov 4:23). The enemy has tricked us into believing that guarding the heart is something we should do in a defensive mode. If we compare it to sports, we can learn a great deal from how games are played. Championship football teams win games by knowing when to run plays defensively and offensively. The defensive line must keep the offensive line from scoring. So, any threat of the offense getting closer to their end zone the defensive line must stop them. When offended, we believe we are protecting ourselves from further injury by blocking or attacking anyone we imagine to be a threat to us. If this defensive strategy becomes the norm, we will successfully build a fortress around the heart, making it cold and hard. The challenge in guarding the heart comes when we don't know when or how to change the play.

When the tactic is changed to offense, the goal is to score, therefore players must be skillful in running plays. The quarterback is the most important offensive position. If he fails to accurately "play and call" the team can lose the game. He must be alert and able to execute good judgment while playing under pressure. It is our task to demonstrate the same skills as it pertains to matters of the heart. We are to control what is allowed to enter the heart so it will remain malleable for growth and maturity.

Given that we are prone to overlook areas of grief and pain, the Lord has made provision for us to ask for His assistance. Jesus told the disciples that God knew them so well that He knew how many strands of hair was on each of their heads (Matt 10:30). Nothing is hidden from God. He is omniscient, meaning that He knows everything about everything and everybody. Our response should be to cry *out "Search me, O God, and know my heart; try me, and know my anxieties"* (Ps 139:23 NKJV). The one who walks in humility greatly benefits by requesting the Lord to inspect him. If we are wise, we learn to embrace the gift of seeing what the Lord sees in our lives. This is a primary step in developing spiritual maturity. Those who continue to reject responsibility for what is revealed to them perceive this information as a threat. If we aren't ready to change, we shouldn't ask God to show us what's there. We must be willing.

Knowing the pathology of the offense is vital to understanding the snare. There are various traps a hunter can use to catch his prey.

If he wanted to catch a bird, he wouldn't use a grounded trap. The bird would be able to see the bait, fly down and remove it without getting caught. To capture a bird, it's best to use a mist net, strung between trees. This way the bird won't see it and fly directly into it. The same trap wouldn't work to capture a deer. In this case, the hunter would use a snare that would cause the animal to be so entangled that it is unable to escape. We find ourselves emotionally entangled when we are not honest and intentional to seek healing of our wounded hearts.

Cause of Stumbling

"If we say that we have fellowship with Him, and walk in darkness, we lie and do not practice the truth."

~ 1John 1:6 NKJV

When the Bible makes inferences to offense, it is typically an illustration of someone being emotionally hurt or injured because of something that has occurred. When we take offense to things done to us, we consider ourselves to be wronged or injured. In a simple world, we look at the things we go through as a work of the enemy, but I beg to differ. The biblical definition of offense means a *"stumbling block or cause of temptation"* (Lk 17:1 NKJV). Ironically, Isaiah says that Jesus would prove to be a source of falling, or tripping. You may wonder how the Prince of Peace can also be labeled a "stumbling block" to man. Israel was known to be disobedient. Unfortunately, they were wayward and rejected Jesus, the Messiah. The One Who is the Chief Cornerstone, or foundation of our faith (1Pe 2:7-8). If we are honest, we are more like Israel than we choose to admit. They seemed to cherish their comfort and sins more than honoring the commandments of God's law. Much like Israel, we often affix a small value to something that God has regarded as costly. This is how we stumble. Instead of walking in the Light of Truth, we choose to look over it in darkness. We sometimes fail at exercising the wisdom it takes to carefully weigh a matter. Despite what is going on around us, let us be mindful that no matter what we face, we can run to the Rock. Jesus is the Prince of Peace and Light of the world (John 8:12).

I remember, after college, when I began living on my own. One night we had a severe thunderstorm and the power went out. When I walked into the kitchen to get my flashlight, I hit my foot on the end table. I knew my way around my apartment and how many steps it took to go from room to room. However, in the darkness I was unable to see what was already there. I stumbled and hit my toe on the side of a table. Jesus' teachings shed light on the dark places in men's lives. His words were convicting people of the truth. They were unable to walk the same way when they were confronted with the dark sin in their lives. The truth they stumbled upon caused many to fall deeper into sin and become harder in heart, which hindered the confrontation of their inner issues. When we are offended, the incident or words spoken are directly linked to something inward and it deserves a thorough investigation. Each of us has inner issues that require us to be mature enough to deal with them.

In righteousness, God was offended by Satan and the world. Knowing the end at the beginning, God knew Satan would not turn away from his rebellion, so it landed him a new home with temporary power. Right now, he is the prince of this world, until the time he will be *"thrown into the lake of fire and sulfur to be tormented forever"* (Rev 20:10 NKJV). Satan continues to be offended and he uses offense to torture unwary believers. We offend God each time we sin, and that sin spiritually separates us from Him (Ro 8:8). This separation is not the will of the Father. He wants us to have intimacy with Him, therefore, He provided forgiveness through the atoning work on the Cross. Nothing else was suitable to satisfy our sin, so God didn't mull over it, instead through Jesus, He brought us back to Himself. The single most powerful sentence in the Bible is John 3:16, *"For God so loved the world, that He gave his only begotten Son, that whosoever believeth in Him should not perish, but have everlasting life"* (NKJV). This single truth dispels the power of offense. The matchless and unwavering love of

God covered the offenses of man when Jesus endured the punishment of our sins against Him.

As Jesus walked out His ministry on earth, He was confronted with a society that intentionally tried to offend Him. It was the spiritual community that offended him the most. These were the people who should have recognized God in His life. Unfortunately, like many of us, they were so steeped in religion and customs that they were unable to recognize the Truth before them. John tells the story of Jesus referencing himself as the Bread of Life. Prior to his conversation, Jesus had already fed the 5,000 with the five fish and two loaves of bread, so they had witnessed His miracles. The same people followed Jesus to Capernaum looking for Him to do something else for them. Knowing this, Jesus corrected them by saying, *"This is the work of God, that you believe in Him whom He sent"* (John 6:29 NKJV). They wanted what He could do for them, but not Him. They wanted to be entertained instead of changed. They refused to accept this information as truth in the face of Jesus. They commented that what was being taught was too difficult for them to do. Many turned away from following Jesus from that point forward. They stumbled.

When Jesus returned to His hometown of Nazareth, He was rejected by those who should have been the first to receive Him. Their offense was focused on their judgment of not wanting to receive from someone like themselves. *"Is not this the carpenter's son?"* (Matt 13:55 NKJV). They questioned how someone they knew could have the wisdom and abilities to do miracles. Perhaps this is a sign of jealousy. The Scripture says they were unable to do many miracles there. *"So, they were offended at Him. But Jesus said to them, "A prophet is not without honor except in his own country and in his own house"* (Matt 13:57 NKJV). Unfortunately, they missed their own blessings. If we are honest with ourselves, we can find ourselves in these verses of Scripture. Jesus is still offending us.

Christians today also fall because of Jesus. Many continue to walk in darkness, tripping over God's Word. They are unable to walk in the Light due to the sins they prefer to hide or cover up. In reality, as they live out their lives, the dark places become more prominent as the Light shines brighter. The pathology of offense requires that every dark and disobedient place in our lives be examined by the Light of Truth. It is our refusal to obey the Truth that causes us to stumble.

Ask yourself:

1. List and explain my plan to guard my heart.
2. What areas of my life need exposing to God's Word?
3. What does the Bible say about the heart?

Pray

Father, I recognize that I have been offended. I have also been an offender. I don't want my feelings and emotions to rule my life any longer. Cleanse my heart and mind and help me to think on the things which are good, true, and of a good report concerning others. I commit myself to You and Your will. In Jesus' name. Amen.

Chapter 5
Symptoms

"While we do not look at the things which are seen, but at the things which are not seen. For the things which are seen are temporary, but the things which are not seen are eternal."

~ 2Corinthians 4:18 NKJV

On occasion, I have noticed my husband a little bent over after one of his early morning basketball games. For years, I have tried to encourage him to put the basketball on the shelf and pick up a golf ball. Needless to say, I continue to lose this battle. When I ask him what's going on with the limp, he responds with a bit of dry sarcasm. I typically shake my head and sarcastically remind him of his intelligence to make good choices concerning his health. Slowly he begins to explain his symptoms. During our annual physicals I'm known to share his recent symptoms with the doctor before he's seen. I do this because Lee won't tell the nurse or doctor what's wrong when he gets in the examination room. Later during the day, I will hear a faint, "Ugh…eew" coming from the closet or down the stairs. Again, using my investigative skills, I will question whether he told the doctor about what he is experiencing. No need to tell you the rest of the story.

Those who are dealing with offense, walk around with symptoms every day. Just like my husband, some will ignore the symptoms despite the pain. To the doctor, symptoms are signs or indicators of what may be manifesting in the body. They are used to rule out some conditions and to confirm others. When the symptoms are obvious and can be seen by others, they are considered to be objective. On the contrary, when others have been told about the symptoms, they are known as subjective. Symptoms are an indicator that something isn't right. If pain is a common gauge of cancer and fever is a sign of infection, without proper attention, the conditions can be fatal. The offended experience an attachment to their pain, which causes their discernment to be dull by the strong sense of self-preservation and anger.

> *"The feeling of being offended is a warning indicator that is showing you where to look within yourself for unresolved issues."*
> ~ Bryant McGill[11]

It is possible for the offended to be unaware of their condition. Early in our marriage my husband told me I sounded like my mother when I said certain things. Of course, I didn't want to hear that, so I passionately responded, "No, I do not sound like my mother!" Our son overheard the conversation and came from the other room and shyly said, "Mom, yes you do. Some stuff you say sounds just like Grandma." Like many teenagers, I vowed to myself that I was not going to say the things my mother said. Well, I did. I was unable to be objective in what I had been saying. My family had listened for a while and they already knew what I had to accept. At that point, I had to decide if I would continue to ignore the symptoms of becoming more like my mom, or if I was going to take authority and change my words. I chose to walk in my authority.

We must keep in mind that all symptoms are not noticeable. Once a person has dealt with a condition for an extended period, there is an inherent danger of accepting the ailment. Remember the man who laid beside the Pool of Bethesda for 38 years in the same condition? This lame man was in the right location, but out of position. When Jesus asked him if he wanted to be well, the man didn't say yes or no. He responded with the excuse he didn't have anyone to help him get in the water. Unaware, this man had accepted his condition despite being in the position to be healed. Many who

---

[11] https://www.azquotes.com/author/9810-Bryant_H_McGill

are infected with the condition of offense have been diagnosed by friends, relatives, and spiritual leaders, yet refuse to confront it. The refusal can have long-lasting and lethal implications. Just like the man at the Pool of Bethesda sacrificed living a productive and satisfying life by clinging to the deck of the pool, those who carry offenses are forfeiting the health of their soul, relationships with others, and compromise their faith in God. (See Appendix B)

Common Symptoms

Sounding like a 'broken record"

People who struggle with being offended will repeat the same issues repeatedly. They tend to tie anything that is similar in nature to their own offense. They appear to have a good memory, but they practice selective recall. The offended easily remember the wrongs they believe have been committed against them. The perceived trauma is like a photo album in the mind.

> **God says…**
> *"Brethren, I do not count myself to have apprehended; but one thing I do, forgetting those things which are behind and reaching forward to those things which are ahead, I press toward the goal for the prize of the upward call of God in Christ Jesus."*
> ~ Philippians 3:13-14 NKJV

Rebellion

People who are in rebellion refuse to yield or bow to authority. This defiance is rooted in pride. They take the position that they aren't accountable to anyone, especially the one who hurt or offended them. The classic biblical picture of rebellion is King David's son, Absalom. David's irresponsible parenting led to Absalom's offense.

David did not confront Amnon's wrongdoing. Those who rebel work passionately to defy established protocol.

> **God says…**
> *"Let this mind be in you which was also in Christ Jesus, who, being in the form of God, did not consider it robbery to be equal with God, but made Himself of no reputation, taking the form of a bondservant, and coming in the likeness of men. And being found in appearance as a man, He humbled Himself and became obedient to the point of death, even the death of the cross."*
> ~ Philippians 2:5-8 NKJV

Withdrawal from relationships and fellowship

The family, community and church are divinely designed for relationship. Ties to others create a sense of strength and belonging. We are meant to bless one another. When we are offended, there is a tendency to pull back or withdraw from the godly relationships around us. It has been said that "isolation is the devil's playground." Many friendships, families and churches have divided because of offense.

> **God says…**
> *"Not forsaking the assembling of ourselves together, as is the manner of some, but exhorting one another, and so much the more as you see the Day approaching."*
> ~ Hebrews 10:25 NKJV

Unresolved Anger

One hindrance to moving beyond offense is anger and none of us are immune to it. If anger settles in our hearts, eventually it will result in some type of negative explosion. This anger doesn't project itself solely at the offender. It is known to affect others also.

God says...
"So then, my beloved brethren, let every man be swift to hear, slow to speak, slow to anger; for the wrath of man does not produce the righteousness of God."

~ James 1:19-20 NKJV

Distrust

Trust is foundational to any relationship. Offense is more difficult to overcome when the offender is someone in whom you have placed a great deal of confidence. Because of the painful brunt of offense, it often leaves you leery of trusting anyone. When it's a leader, it may cause the offended to lose trust in all leaders and authority figures. Rather than placing relationships in God's hands, this person becomes cynical, detached and self-sufficient.

God says...
"Have I not commanded you? Be strong and of good courage; do not be afraid, nor be dismayed, for the Lord your God is with you wherever you go."

~ Joshua 1:9 NKJV

Resentment

When a person has a bitter hurt towards someone, he is resentful. This happens when an offense has lingered for a lengthy period. Ironically, resentment attacks the one holding the resentment. It is the devil's strategy to hold you in bondage to yesterday. A sure way to miss today's gift is to remain in the pains of yesterday.

God says...
"Looking carefully lest anyone fall short of the grace of God; lest any root of bitterness springing up cause trouble, and by this many become defiled."

~ Hebrews 12:15 NKJV

Betrayal

An offense can lead to betrayal or a betrayal may be the cause of offense. Either way, betrayal is a violation of trust between two people, presumably friends. This offense creates inner and outer relational friction. Merriam-Webster suggests betrayal to be a revelation of something hidden or secret. Therefore, the power of betrayal comes as a gut punch that can bring you to your knees because it destroys the confidence once had in a relationship.

God says…

"He who goes about as a talebearer reveals secrets; therefore, do not associate with one who flatters with his lips."

~ Proverbs 25:9-10 NLT

"And whenever you stand praying, if you have anything against anyone, forgive him, that your Father in heaven may also forgive you your trespasses."

~ Mark 11:25 NKJV

Unanswered Prayers

When we pray, we are seeking divine intervention in the affairs of our lives. Releasing the offense unblocks the blessings. The Psalmist says, *"If I regard iniquity in my heart the Lord does not hear me"* (Ps 66:18 NKJV).

God says…

"Take heed, do not turn to iniquity, for you have chosen this rather than affliction."

~Job 36:21 NKJV

"For if you forgive men their trespasses, your heavenly Father will also forgive you."

~ Matthew 6:14 NKJV

Self-Righteous

The person who is unable to see their flaws but has a clear view of their offender's flaws is self-righteous. We must accept that no one is perfect, and all have areas that must be submitted to the lordship of Jesus Christ, even the most holy of us. Even if you are the one who was least in contributing to the demise of a relationship, it does not excuse you from the Christian obligation to forgive.

> **God says...**
> *"Judge not, and you shall not be judged. Condemn not, and you shall not be condemned. Forgive, and you will be forgiven."*
>
> ~ Luke 6:37 NKJV

Gossip about the offender

When we are hurt by someone, it is natural to want the hurt to be returned. The enemy uses the offense to influence us to gossip about the offender. It can be the hardest to resist telling what you know about them, whether it's true or not. Gossiping about others has a way of initially bringing temporary satisfaction. It ultimately destroys your reputation and relationships with those you have gossiped to.

> **God says...**
> *"Let no corrupt word proceed out of your mouth, but what is good for necessary edification, that it may impart grace to the hearers."*
>
> ~ Ephesians 4:29 NKJV

Viewing the Offender as an enemy

We are all susceptible to offend another person without the intention to harm. If you view someone who hurt your feelings as being an enemy, chances are you are dealing with offense. It isn't God's will that we harbor ill will towards one another, with or without cause.

> **God says...**
> *"When people's lives please the Lord, even their enemies are at peace with them."*
>
> ~ Proverbs 16:7 NLT

> *"No, O people, the Lord has told you what is good, and this is what He requires of you: to do what is right, to love mercy, and to walk humbly with your God."*
>
> ~ Micah 6:8 NLT

Unforgiveness

The person bound to unforgiveness will show some or all the above-named symptoms. This negative choice is toxic to the soul with one means of cure: forgiveness.

> **God says...**
> *"If My people who are called by My name will humble themselves, and pray and seek My face, and turn from their wicked ways, then I will hear from heaven, and will forgive their sin and heal their land."*
>
> ~ 2Chronicles 7:14 NKJV

> *"Blessed are the merciful, for they shall obtain mercy."*
>
> ~ Matthew 5:7 NKJV

Ask yourself:

1. What symptoms of offense do I have in my life?
2. List and describe how the symptoms affect my thinking and decisions.
3. What is the importance of "fixing my eyes on Jesus?"

Pray

Father, I don't want to live in offense. It is not my desire to ignore anything that hinders me from living in the freedom You have provided. Help me to be honest with myself so that I may have the inner peace, joy, and good relationships with others. In Jesus' name. Amen.

Chapter 6
Forgiveness

"Should you not also have had compassion on your fellow servant, just as I had pity on you?"

~ Matthew 18:33 NKJV

A divine relationship exists between unforgiveness and offense, therefore the symptoms are very similar. When we choose to forgive from the heart, offense loses its power. It's simple. If you know that God requires that we forgive others and you say you forgive, then the decision cannot remain a choice of the intellect, it must source from the heart. The intellectual justification is not enough to sustain our souls. The soul has a remarkable ability to connect experiences. People are biologically designed with a mind, will and emotions, making them prone to emotional responses. Forgiving someone who has offended you is a choice, but how you process the forgiveness is typically attached to some type of feeling and emotion.

Our souls hold the ingredients of our life experiences. At the first sign of cold weather, I like to make a pot of soup. It is always a reminder of growing up and hearing my dad compliment my mother's homemade vegetable soup. He would say, "Evelyn, that was a good pot." He was not saying the literal pot was good; he was referring to its contents. Our soul is like the pot. I have learned the secret to a great tasting pot of soup is found in simmering. If I boil water with fresh vegetables, browned beef, salt and pepper, I couldn't expect anyone to eat it because of the bland taste. However, if I boil the fresh vegetables and browned meat in beef stock, reduce it to a simmer and refrigerate it for four hours, the taste is delectable! The process of simmering and cooling allows the flavors to penetrate in the ingredients. Then, when the pot is reheated, any remaining unwanted water is evaporated in the reheating. In the same way, the soul is a stock pot filled with life's thoughts, experiences, joys, pains, losses and gains. The simmering process causes penetration. When we simmer the offense, it becomes more difficult to forgive because it has saturated the mind and heart.

Think about it this way. Romans 10:9 tells us to *"confess with our mouths and believe with our hearts."* If the confession of faith comes from the intellect alone, it simply means that a person believes what they say is the logical route to take in order to miss going to hell. In this illustration, the heart has not made the connection. Therefore, it becomes easy to return to old ways because the person had merely selected an alternative method for the time. He is literally "caught up" in the moment without commitment. This is because the heart has not been renewed.

Regenerate
"re" – prefix
- means again or renew
"generate" – transitive verb
- to bring into existence[12]

Spiritually, regeneration simply implies rebirth. So, Ezekiel prophesies, *"I will give you a new heart, and I will put a new spirit in you. I will take out your stony, stubborn heart and give you a tender, responsive heart. And I will put my Spirit in you so that you will follow my decrees and be careful to obey my regulations"* (Ez 36:26-27 NLT). The stony heart being replaced with the new and tender heart is regeneration. It is interesting to note that regeneration is needed when there has been an injury, damage or disease. When you believe with your heart there is a settled conviction, an inner knowing that God is within and persuading you toward righteousness and truth. That inner conviction is felt so intensely that

---

[12] https://www.merriam-webster.com/dictionary/regenerate

it will compel you to want to do what is right. It will also convict you when you know you are doing wrong. When you sincerely forgive the offender, you are not denying the violation, you are trusting God's power and handing it over to Him. This is honoring the lordship of Christ. We must trust God over self. If you are unable to embrace this concept, consider what Paul shared with the Ephesian Church.

> *"For this reason, I bow my knees to the Father of our Lord Jesus Christ, from whom the whole family in heaven and earth is named, that He would grant you, according to the riches of His glory, to be strengthened with might through His Spirit in the inner man, that Christ may dwell in your hearts through faith; that you, being **rooted and grounded** in love, may be able to comprehend with all the saints what is the width and length and depth and height— to know the love of Christ which passes knowledge; that you may be filled with all the fullness of God. Now to Him who is able to do exceedingly abundantly above all that we ask or think, according to the power that works in us, to Him be glory in the church by Christ Jesus to all generations, forever and ever. Amen."*
> ~ Ephesians 3:14-20 NKJV

Paul, who once was an offender, became the offended. As an offender, his eyes were veiled, or covered, so that he could not see the truth of who Jesus was and His work. I remember being in Jamaica having dinner at a restaurant that would catch the fish and bring it to your table before cooking it. The waiter was delighted with my choice and proceeded to tell me how much I would enjoy it. As he was describing the taste of the fish, I was saying to myself, "Please get that thing cleaned so I can eat it." I smiled, nodded my head and let him talk. I couldn't enjoy the delicacy of that fish until the outer layer was removed, neither could Paul see until the layer of scales were removed from his eyes. When the scales fell, it was symbolic of his conversion. The transformation was a supernatural encounter with the Lord. He was knocked down and led in the path of righteousness.

Prior to Paul's Damascus Road conversion, he had given no thought outside of his Pharisaic teachings. In Paul's evil stead, he believed he was working for Jehovah God. He was convinced and very proud of his record of evil intent. He muses, *"Although I was formerly a blasphemer, a persecutor, and an insolent man; but I obtained mercy because I did it ignorantly in unbelief"* (1Tim 1:13 NKJV). Paul recognized he was previously living outside the will of God. He was committed to false doctrine. He was serving teachings contrary to the character of God, Who is love. We are to be rooted and grounded in love, always looking to the face of Jesus. When we were still in sin, He offered forgiveness. I rejoice in Paul's prayer for God's strength to do what he could not do. He writes, *"Now to Him who is able to do exceedingly abundantly above all that we ask or think, according to the power that works in us"* (Eph 3:20 NKJV). Paul had to forgive and be forgiven. As a persecutor, he offended many and after he accepted Christ he stood in need of forgiveness. He had to go back to the people with whom he had once caused harm. They judged his integrity and the validity of his stance.

In his weakness, Jesus prayed, *"Father, forgive them, for they do not know what they do"* (Lk 23:34 NKJV). He was fully aware of what was ahead and how he would be treated – without cause, yet he asked for Heaven's assistance. We know the Lord walked a perfect life, without sin, but He felt what we feel and He held fast to the principle of love. For us as Christ-followers, Christians, born-again believers, forgiveness is an undeniable command. *"And be kind to one another, tenderhearted, forgiving one another, even as God in Christ forgave you"* (Eph 4:32 NKJV). Be mindful that our forgiveness is not contingent upon whether the offender has acknowledged or apologized for their wrong. It's not about them, it is about you and God.

"We must develop and maintain the capacity to forgive.
He who is devoid of the power to forgive is devoid of the power to love.

*There is some good in the worst of us and some evil in the best of us.
When we discover this, we are less prone to hate our enemies."*
~ Martin Luther King, Jr.[13]

Sin is part of our human nature; therefore, we don't have to be taught to walk in unforgiveness. On the contrary, we must be taught to forgive. Two of my favorite biblical heroes refer to the struggle of sin. King David asserts, *"Behold, I was brought forth in iniquity, and in sin my mother conceived me"* (Ps 51:5 NKJV). He clearly recognized that he had a nature that had a proclivity to sin. He wasn't excusing it but acknowledging his tendency to miss the mark of the Lord's standard. Centuries later, the Apostle Paul declares, *"So then, with the mind I myself serve the law of God, but with the flesh the law of sin"* (Ro 7:25 NKJV). Here, Paul is being very transparent, literally admitting that it is much easier to know the Word than it is to walk it out. Neither men used their significance in God to deny their susceptibility to fall short of the glory of God. Neither should we.

*"For the mature, you value your mind, energy and virtue, so choosing
to forgive is the easiest and strongest decision you will ever make."*
~ Margo W. Williams

Another example is the Corinthian church. They were known to be wealthy, gifted and carnally minded. Satan successfully came in and appealed to their immaturity. He persuaded them to continue living as they had done prior to their faith confession. In the context of forgiveness, Paul knew this, and he warned the Corinthians to forgive one another *"lest Satan should take advantage of us; for we are not ignorant of his devices"* (2Cor 2:11 NKJV). Satan loves to see believers struggle with forgiveness because it is a great tool of division. When there is unity, God can do extraordinary works in our lives individually and collectively.

---

[13] https://www.penguinrandomhouse.ca/books/212014/a-gift-of-love-by-martin-luther-king-jr/9780807000632/excerpt

In many ways, the believer is a model for the world. If you're like me, on occasion I have purchased an outfit because I admired the way it looked on someone else or in an advertisement. A couple of times I made the buy before seeing if it fit. Once home, I tried it on and was disappointed with how it looked on me. Of course, I returned it, but it taught me there were some areas of my body that needed to be perfected in order to model the look I was after. Jesus' walk of forgiveness is the model we are to follow. Despite our current conditions, the salvation of Christ provides forgiveness for our past, present and future sins. It is written, *"For He made Him who knew no sin to be sin for us, that we might become the righteousness of God in Him."* (2Cor. 5:21 NKJV). Jesus paid it all. If we find that forgiving others does not fit us well, then we need to get our bodies in shape so we can look like the Devine Advertisement, Jesus.

I would like to caution you that it is possible to believe you have forgiven a person when in reality you haven't. Sin is clever in keeping us bound to theories of self-awareness while ignoring self-preservation. Self-awareness is to be in-touch with the inner self. It is not enough to recognize the character flaws, impure motives, negative feelings and toxic behaviors, you must take action. You must be willing to interrogate yourself for the purpose of becoming your best self. The one who is resigned to self-preservation recognizes what should be dealt with, but he chooses to protect the thing that ought to be destroyed. King David prayed, *"Search me, O God, and know my heart; try me, and know my anxieties; and see if there is any wicked way in me, and lead me in the way everlasting"* (Ps 139:23-24 NKJV).

That Place

"Being confident of this very thing, that He who has begun a good work in you will complete it until the day of Jesus Christ."
~ Philippians 1:6 NKJV

There are many benefits to forgiving others. Perhaps you are the person who admits, "I'm not there yet," but would like to get there. This is not an uncommon place, neither is it an indictment. Before you condemn yourself for struggling to forgive, consider that God has given us insight into the lives of His people. Many biblical characters struggled with getting to "that place," but God used them anyway. Before we are conceived God has already ordained the purpose for our lives, therefore when He looks at us He sees our future beyond the present. For various reasons, we are seldom able to see what God sees. That lack of vision works to slow down our process. The most efficient route to "that place" is to partner with God. With each character in the Bible, God proved to be faithful time and time again.

The book of Proverbs was written to impart wisdom in the life of the believer. With this in mind, people are regarded as being simple, wise or foolish in their decisions. No where will you find advice to the half-way or "not ready" audience. As you explore the entire book, you will discover advice that is precisely black or white, right or wrong. Note that the simple are the young and immature. This is a stage everyone must go through on the way to maturity. During this stage of life, a person is vulnerable to the influence of the wise and the foolish. Proverbs 1:4 says, *"These proverbs will give insight to the simple, knowledge and discernment to the young"* (NKJV). Because we all must travel the road of simplicity, we are destined to reach maturity. On the way, some take exits – or detours – down the foolish highway. Paul describes the simple as the carnal minded. The father who is teaching his son in Proverbs 1, instructs him that as he matures, he must make the choice in how he wants to be identified: the wise or the foolish (Prov 1:10, 15, 22-23). The simple can be easily influenced to do wrong and make dangerous decisions (Prov 14:15, 22:3).

The second type of believers are noted to be foolish. These are the people who trust in their own minds rather than God's Word (Prov 28:26), as we know that the foundation of our beliefs is built upon what we believe about God. This principle is worthy of caution because it has the power to influence every facet of life. Then there are the wise. As a parent, I tried to counsel our children to be mindful of their futures as it relates to their present decisions. In following Jesus' teachings, I wanted to instill the wisdom of being prepared and counting the cost of their choices (Matt 7:24-27). Jesus uses an analogy that paints a vivid picture of the outcomes of the wise and the foolish. Traditionally, wisdom has been defined as the practical application of knowledge. This means that once you gain knowledge of truth, the evidence of your understanding is found in how you apply that knowledge in life. A distinct line separates the wise from the foolish.

On the road to" that place" you must decide which road you will follow. God is gracious, merciful and righteous. He gives us the right to choose for ourselves the trajectory of living. In my life I have learned that the Lord's way is straight, but it's filled with mountains and valleys, deserts and rivers, however, He uses every terrain to build faith and character. In other words, sometimes choosing wisdom may not be the easy route. God has a plan to get you to "that place" and He knows what is waiting for you there. If you have not arrived at "that place" each time you whisper a "yes" to the Lord, the journey gets shorter. The wise road that leads to life is paved with forgiveness. Forgiveness is a decision. You choose.

"If you refuse to obey the Word, you deceive your own heart."
~ Margo W. Williams

Testimony

Several years ago, I knew a woman who was suffering from allergies and asthma. She had repeatedly visited her doctor and her condition seemed to worsen. Most of her tests were inconclusive and she asked me to intercede for her as it pertained to her physical health. I agreed to pray and within days, the Holy Spirit gave me a clear image of a vine being wrapped around her neck. At first, I was uncertain what it meant, and I continued to pray for her as she had asked. Later, the Lord revealed that she was filled with anger and resentment towards some of her family. When I spoke with her about what I had seen she responded with a stare, not offering any verbal response. I told her that when she forgives whoever she was angry with that her breathing issues would clear up. For weeks, I noticed there wasn't any improvement. About four months later, she told me that someone else had told her the same thing I had shared earlier, and that she had forgiven her family members. At that time, her health was improving greatly, and she had reunited with her siblings.

Thinking back, when this woman walked in unforgiveness she appeared to be distracted, sad, and distant with people. She didn't know it, but I continued to watch her life and how she had changed. I noticed she had begun smiling and interacting with others again. Her experience is a testimony of the power of love and forgiveness. Although she harbored resentment toward certain family members, I believe she also loved them as best as she could, given her heart's condition. Her love was being strangled by years of unresolved misunderstandings, tensions and unforgiveness. I also observed this woman to have a contentious and controlling nature when things did not go her way. Her refusal to forgive created an invisible wall between her heart and mind so that she would feel protected in her misery. She had allowed issues of her past to construct a toxic prison of bitterness in her life. Satan reasoned and she agreed that she had every right to feel and behave the way she did because of all she believed they had done to her.

This situation is a clear picture of the power of love and forgiveness. No matter what we experience, the potency of God's love in our lives is tested by our willingness to forgive others – whether they are deserving or not. In fact, the one who does not love is unable to forgive.

Ask yourself:

1. Explain what it means to forgive from the heart.

2. Who am I refusing to forgive? What has caused me to "hold on" to the offense?
3. Describe what it means for me to ask God to search me?

Pray

Father, I thank You that You are not like me. You have given me grace and mercy; therefore, I am to give others what I have received from You. I simply ask that You help me to forgive, in the same way Christ has forgiven me. In Jesus' name. Amen.

Chapter 7
TRAPS

"We escaped like a bird from a hunter's trap. The trap is broken, and we are free!"

~ Psalm 124:7 NLT

Any good hunter knows how to set the right trap to catch a prey. The fisherman understands the bait must be palatable for the catch he is wanting to hook. Satan has studied our nature, so he knows how to provoke, or trap us in his hold. Surely his knowledge is limited, but he is a patient foe that has an army of support behind him. He will study our ways to find out the areas of our strengths and weaknesses. This strategy works well because he does not want to fight to gain his victim, he would rather that the victim yield to the threat of his power. Peter reminds us, *"Be sober, be vigilant; because your adversary, the devil, walks about like a roaring lion, seeking whom he may devour. Resist him, steadfast in the faith, knowing that the same sufferings are experienced by your brotherhood in the world"* (1Pe 5:8-9 NKJV).

Timing is Everything

"To everything there is a season, a time for every purpose under heaven"

~ Ecclesiastes 3:1 NKJV

The book of First Chronicles refers to the Sons of Issachar who knew how to discern the times. What does this mean? Discerning the times is a way of saying you understand what is happening and you know how to respond to it. This understanding is sourced from the Holy Spirit and emanates from within, not depending on an outside source to reveal it to you. We grow in discernment the more consistent and intimate we are in our worship and prayer to the Lord. The same holds true for the avid sportsman, through consistent observation and practice, he knows the best times for the catch. A good fisherman takes note of the season and temperatures to know the best time to cast the net. The same is true for deer hunters. It is interesting to note that deer are intuitive of their surroundings, so they protect themselves from animal predators by staying awake all night and sleeping in the daytime. Sportsmen have learned to capitalize by hunting deer in the early morning hours. This way, the deer are vulnerable because they are tired and sleepy from wandering all night.

The enemy of our souls does his best work when he can catch us off guard. The Bible proposes that God does not want us to be ignorant of the enemy's schemes, otherwise he would take advantage of us. Instead, we are to *"be sober and vigilant,"* prepared for whatever the enemy tries to do (1Pe 5:8). He should not be able to catch us off-guard. Like the deer hunter, the enemy is looking for the best circumstances to lay his snare. Peter says the devil is seeking his prey. He is studying our lives, looking for the attitudes, desires, and weaknesses. Once the conditions are favorable, he can trap us. There are many believers who invest heavily in their stance of being strong minded and relentless in what they believe. This mindset is also what the enemy is depending on. He knows that the more rigid a believer is in their own abilities, the easier they are to be ensnared. The one whose mind is settled on self is not resting in God. *"He who trusts in his own heart is a fool, but whoever walks wisely will be delivered"* (Prov 28:26 NKJV).

Another key component to being snared is evidenced by the times in which we are living. Jesus is noted for sharing eight signs that would signal the End of the Age and offense is one of them. *"And then many will be offended, will betray one another, and will hate one another"* (Matt 24:10 NKJV). If you are having a difficult time dealing with offense, then I ask that you consider the timing of this issue.

Begin by asking yourself these questions: "Do I have time? Is it worth it?" Jesus is going to return and take us back with Him. He is also going to read our divine report card in Heaven. The enemy is aware he does not have the power to take your salvation, but he is confident he is able to destroy your character and witness. Spiritual character isn't based on your reputation in church, it is built upon the motives of your heart and your actions. *"For we must all appear before the judgment seat of Christ, that each one may receive the things done in the body, according to what he has done, whether good or bad"* (2Cor 5:10 NKJV). Every one of us will have to answer to the Lord for everything we have done while on earth – good and bad. It won't benefit us to point fingers and offer petty excuses for doing wrong. He knows everything and He will judge it.

We should not confuse working with works. The inner workings of the Holy Spirit produce the Fruit of the Spirit. This cluster of fruit is held in place by God's generous basket of grace. That grace is a compelling force, which encourages us to honor the Lord in how we treat everyone, not only those you attend church with, or share family blood. To the Lord, our obedience is proven in our attitude and behavior toward others and His Word. How believers handle themselves is divinely monitored. God holds our ways up to the standard of His Word; therefore, He is not biased in how He judges. No amount of working in the church or community can replace the fruits of righteousness. It is the Lord who will ultimately settle life issues with each person. *"But glory, honor, and peace to everyone who works what is good, to the Jew first and also to the Greek. For there is no partiality with God"* (Ro 2:10-11 NKJV). The purity test of all we do begins with the posture of the heart.

> *"When my spirit was overwhelmed within me, then You knew my path. In the way in which I walk they have secretly set a snare for me."*
>
> ~Psalm 142:3 NKJV

In their natural habitat, animals are free to roam. Although the animal kingdom is dangerous, they instinctively know how to protect themselves from other animals in the wild. When man has studied wild creatures, he becomes skillful in capturing them for commerce, food, sport, and safety. The best hunters know how to discreetly lay a snare without the animal recognizing that it is there. If an animal is caught and tries to get away it is unable to escape. The Psalmist declares, *"Great peace have those who love Your law, and nothing causes them to stumble"* (Ps 119:165 NKJV). The Hebrew word translated offend is *"mikshol"* (mik-shole').[14] It means a stumbling block or something that causes you to fall.

As stated earlier, the snare is not intended to kill the animal. When a person is snared by an offense, he literally stumbles on something that is laying down in front of him that he cannot or is unwilling to look at. I say this because being offended is a choice. What has been said or done should not have power over us. If a person chooses to be offended by the actions of another, then they have agreed with the offender. When the person chooses not to be offended, they have rejected the offense. In other words, no one has the power to make you offended. You always have the option of rejecting or receiving an offense. You have a choice. The receipt of an offense means that something is present or lying within you. The enemy is clever in how he orchestrates an offense. He realizes he does not have to work hard to cause you to fall if you ignore what is already there. If you are insecure, overly sensitive, arrogant, and easily embarrassed, then he knows how to place something before you to provoke a negative reaction.

Look at it this way: The phrase "lying within" is the bait the enemy uses to trap you into the prison of offense. As you walk through life, be careful where you step, or you can walk into a trap. If caught in the trap, it can hinder your ability to walk with a steady gait. It has the potential to trap or paralyze you from moving forward. Be mindful that Satan lays the trap, not the one you believe has

---

[14] https://www.blueletterbible.org/lang/lexicon/lexicon.cfm?t=kjv&strongs=h4383

offended you. It is petty to allow a person to take the blame for the enemy's work.

Snare-Trap

"That they might go, and fall backward, and be broken, and snared, and caught."

~ Isaiah 28:13 NKJV

Snare[15]	Trap[16]
verb \ ˈsner \	verb \ ˈtrap \
1. Something deceptively attractive	1. to catch or take in
2. Entice and trap	2. to place in a restricted position

I have fond memories of our parents and how both appreciated nature and wildlife. As a little girl, I spent many summer evenings with my mom and one of her friends, sitting on the bank of a pond in the middle of a cow pasture. They would tell me not to look at the cows and to "hold it down" so the fish would not get away. Sometimes I would cast my pole or little Zebco Rod and Reel. Usually Mom or Mrs. Margaret would bait the hook for me, but one day they told me to do it myself. "What?" Momma said, "If you want to catch something today, then you're gonna have to bait that hook. If you don't want to use the worms, use the corn or livers." I skipped the worms for the corn. They looked at the hook and instructed me to completely cover it with the corn so the fish couldn't see the metal. I obeyed, cast the line and got a bite! Without the corn to lure the fish, I would have gone home without a catch. The corn was used to snare or lure the fish to the hook.

---

[15] https://www.merriam-webster.com/dictionary/snare
[16] https://www.merriam-webster.com/dictionary/trap

My fishing story relates to the snares of the enemy. Not only was I taught to use bait, but I learned that different species were drawn to different kinds of bait. If I wanted to catch crappie, I would use the minnows and for the bream I had to use the worms or crickets. The enemy uses a type of bait to snare people in the trap of offense. Be mindful that he masterfully uses deception as his snare or bait of choice. Deception is only successful when it has the power to intimidate your thinking. It has an invisible venom that permeates the mind and flows through the heart. Isaiah describes this illness as causing people to stumble backwards or turn themselves away from what they know is the truth. As it travels through the body, a brokenness occurs causing them to deny what they once knew to be true. By this time, the deception has successfully ensnared the victims and they are taken away by their sin and prideful hearts. Instead of adhering to God's Word, they become victims of their own rebellion.

Many believers experience torment because snares of the flesh have trapped them. They sin against one another and hinder God's Kingdom destiny for their lives. Unfortunately, these same believers live as *"whitewashed tombs"* (Matt 23:27). They waste time perfecting their outer appearance while their inside is wasting away. The Lord wants us to live with the inward and outer beauty that reveals His kingdom and not allow ourselves to be ensnared into traps.

Snare 1 – Wrong Assumptions

"Therefore, let us not judge one another anymore, but rather resolve this, not to put a stumbling block or a cause to fall in our brother's way."

~ Romans 14:13 NKJV

When we assume about someone or their intentions, we are choosing to be oblivious to the truth. How many times have you concluded to know someone or something without having all the details? Have you ever been told someone said something and you decided you knew their heart? Even when you felt convicted and asked for clarity, you held fast to your assumption of what was intended. Perhaps your conclusion of matters is based on your past unresolved issues. When we assume we know what someone means, we are essentially saying that we will not consider anything outside of how we view the situation. Most often, this unfair and narrow perspective is an emotional response fueled by unresolved disappointments, hurts, or pride. Sadly, more difficulty is created when we make false assumptions. This snare works very well to produce bitterness and resentment toward others, all while being unfounded.

> *"Do not judge according to appearance, but judge with righteous judgment."*
>
> ~ John 7:24 NKJV

This age is enamored with the prospect that no one has sincere motives. This attitude produces distrust. Ironically, the one who does not trust others is also being viewed as not being trustworthy. This is a sad commentary for the church. Each of us has experienced a situation or conversation that sounded like "shade," but in reality, was a simple misunderstanding. Over the years, the meaning of many words has changed without generational and academic notice. For example, I can remember when I described something as being nasty because it tasted terrible. Today, something referred to as being nasty and dirty is an urban compliment. Too often we become concerned about non-issues. With offense, we have the power to choose our position. We can choose to believe an issue is present, we can choose to ignore the issue, or we can choose to believe there really is not an issue of offense. Of the three options, the question of whether any of them are accurate is contained in the rooted reason, or core issue.

When we assume something, we make a judgment without investigating the validity of the matter. With offense, we assume a word or action without gathering and considering all the facts. It should be noted that facts alone are not an exact determination of truth. Truth yields higher honor than facts do. For example, I can assume my neighbor doesn't like me because he never waves his hand or utters a friendly "good morning" when we see each other in the driveway. If I see the same neighbor at the community grocery store talking and laughing with another neighbor who lives four houses down the street, I am offended. From the lack of communication between him and myself, I believe the neighbor dislikes me. Later, I learn the neighbor's wife suffers with paranoia due to PTSD. Due to this condition, her husband refrains from associating with anyone until his wife has met them and she believes they aren't a perceived threat. On the surface this is superficial, but below the surface there is a major problem. If we automatically assume the worst about others intentions, it causes unnecessary stress and strain. There is a larger issue speaking. "Why is it so important to be 'liked' by others?" By assuming we know someone's heart we blatantly disregard the possibility of being incorrect.

Snare 2 – Refusal to Acknowledge You're Wrong

> *"Do you see a man wise in his own eyes? There is more hope for a fool than for him."*
>
> ~ Proverbs 26:12 NKJV

No one is right all the time and the enemy would love for us to bask in our ignorance. When we are offended because we do not acknowledge someone else as being right, we are wrestling with ourselves. It says that we would rather uphold the consequences of being wrong rather than humble ourselves and honor truth. This attitude will certainly lead to dissatisfaction and turmoil. There can be no peace when we knowingly betray ourselves for the sake of pride and arrogance. In the C.S. Lewis classic, *Mere Christianity*, he writes, "A proud man is always looking down on things and people; and, of course, as long as you are looking down, you cannot see something that is above you."[17] When we have a healthy perspective of ourselves, we are apt to be positive and encouraging to others. Our viewpoint may be to withhold acknowledgement of others because we did not receive affirmation from those we cared the most about. Unfortunately, this is a sure sign of inner sickness.

There is a Native American proverb which says, "Never criticize a man until you've walked a mile in his moccasins." There is always the choice to consider the other side. This act of the will requires one to step outside of themselves and truly examine the other person's perspective. When we ask the Holy Spirit to reveal them to us, He has a sweet way of causing us to see what we couldn't earlier.

Snare 3 – Refusal to Look Within

"Search me, O God, and know my heart; try me, and know my anxieties."

~ Psalm 139:23 NKJV

One of the greatest struggles we have is to face what we do not like about ourselves. Let's face it, it is so much easier to look outwardly instead of inwardly. Life is much easier if we play the proverbial blame game. We are somewhat wired to believe the best of ourselves and less of others. This breeds the misfortune of not discovering the reason we are offended. This excavation suggests that we remove the thin shroud of perfection and expose ourselves to the Light. *"Then I saw that wisdom excels folly as light excels darkness"* (Ecc 2:13 NKJV). When we ask the Lord to reveal what is hidden in our souls, we discern the substance of our darkness. It is only then that we are able to confront what we really believe about ourselves. *"For as he thinks in his heart, so is he"* (Prov 23:7 NKJV). If we believe we will be disliked, rejected, not enough, not smart, ugly, then our lives will give

---

[17] https://www.goodreads.com/quotes/9707-a-proud-man-is-always-looking-down-on-things-and

in to what we have chosen to accept. These negative thoughts are doors to our self-image, esteem, insecurities, and the need to compare and compete. In reality, there is a silent inner desire for outside approval.

The low view of self will cause us to quickly run to our own defense. This is identified by the exaggeration of others' opinions and behaviors. On the contrary, it may be an inflated view of self. If we dare to be truthful, those who refuse to look at themselves use themselves as the measure for others to follow. Earlier generations described them as being high-minded or full of pride. This lofty and unchallenged view of self is a sure pathway for strife. The Holman Christian Standard Bible translation of Philippians 2:3 says, *"Do nothing out of rivalry or conceit, but in humility consider others as more important than yourselves."* Walking in pride is the front-runner of backbiting, holding grudges, impatience, and jealousy. Another inflammatory agent can be the ego. According to the Cambridge Dictionary, ego is defined as the idea or opinion that we have of ourselves, particularly as it relates to our individual sense of importance, intellect and capabilities.

Snare 4 – Lack of Appreciation For Others

"Now may the God of patience and comfort grant you to be like-minded toward one another, according to Christ Jesus."
~ Romans 15:5 NKJV

It's easy to be snared when you have very little appreciation for other people in your life. This means we take relationships for granted. Anything we value, we cherish, and we try to keep it safe. If you appreciate your relationships, then you are less likely to remain offended. The value we place on those relationships we care about helps us to confront the offense within self and with others. Having a lack of appreciation for others can be attached to attitudes that hinder gratitude. For example, a person with a bend toward jealousy, greed, narcissism, suspicion, sarcasm, and materialism may have a difficult time with placing others in a position of true importance. Author Melody Beattie says, "Gratitude unlocks the fullness of life. It turns what we have into enough, and more. It turns denial into acceptance, chaos to order, confusion to clarity. It can turn a meal into a feast, a house into a home, a stranger into a friend."[18]

Everyone desires to be valued and appreciated in life. People who struggle with being grateful must overcome their fascination with self and welcome others in the door of their lives. This means they must be willing to respect and consider others' views and opinions. *"So then, those who are in the flesh cannot please God"* (Ro 8:8 NKJV). People who are absorbed with themselves seldom make room for others unless it is for personal gain in some way. We are designed to bless and serve others. This certainly demands that we appreciate who God places in our lives. *"Let each of you look out not only for his own interests, but also for the interests of others"* (Phil 2:4 NKJV).

Snare 5 – Lack of Self-Acceptance

"And He said to me, 'My grace is sufficient for you, for My strength is made perfect in weakness.' Therefore, most gladly I will rather boast in my infirmities, that the power of Christ may rest upon me."

~ 2Corinthians 12:9 NKJV

In the private spaces of our minds, we reserve thoughts of ourselves that we seldom, if ever, discuss with others. These places whisper misunderstandings, accusations, harsh criticisms and abuses to our souls. Those words work together to construct a mirror of insecurities, doubts, fears, and self-rejection. Through years of rehearsal, the enemy uses this marred self-image to deter or cause us to reject others with or without cause. It is a masterful plan to hinder us from

---

[18] https://www.goodreads.com/author/quotes/4482.Melody_Beattie

establishing healthy relationships with other people. If we fail to recognize ourselves by God's image for us, then we are apt to accept the enemy's perspective. Jesus said we are to love our neighbors as ourselves (Matt 22:39). This commandment assumes that we have a healthy view of who we are.

When our lens are cloudy, we are unable to see ourselves and others clearly. Both must be brought into focus. Without clear visual acuity, our esteem is obstructed and we self-reject by devaluing our worth, quieting our voice, and accepting the worse. Although we may never discuss these areas with anyone, when they are brought to our attention, it's like placing them under a magnifying lens. Inviting the Holy Spirit to strengthen us in our weak places, produces the power we need to overcome issues within ourselves. We must learn to accept that we are all perfect in our imperfections. At no time are we to condemn others and excuse our wrongs. Accepting ourselves for who we are opens the door for us to forgive.

Snare 6 - Poor Communication

"A word fitly spoken is like apples of gold in settings of silver."
~ Proverbs 25:11 NKJV

One of the easiest ways to be offended is bad communication. Speaking without thinking can be a way that we easily become the offender or the offended. Whether the offense is caused by what is said, who said it, or how it was said, there can be lasting effects. As I have journeyed through life, I have found that wounds from words can take years to heal. Too often we will say something that should have been left unspoken. This is a lack of self-control with the tongue. Growing up, the follow-up for offensive attacks was, "Sticks and stones may break my bones, but words can never hurt me." Even for the toughest kid on the playground, invariably you could see a change in physical posture and mood when hateful things would be directed at him. This verbal offense also reveals itself when one is lied on or misled.

This snare is most effective with people who deny that an offense exists while inwardly feeling embarrassed, upset, disparaged or intimidated. Inadvertently they will say, "I'm good. I don't even care what they said about me." On the outside these words appear to be a sign of strength, so they will exist in a prison of denial where each offensive word serves as bars that keep them bound. Paul warned, *"Let no corrupt word proceed out of your mouth, but what is good for necessary edification, that it may impart grace to the hearers."* (Eph 4:29 NKJV).

Snare 7 – Fatigue/Stress

"Cast your burden on the Lord, and He shall sustain you;
He shall never permit the righteous to be moved."

~ Psalm 55:22 NKJV

In this age, many are guilty of stretching ourselves beyond our ability to be effective. There is a constant drive to get all we can, as quickly as we can, for as long as we can. This is the inevitable method for success. While I believe in mastering anything I decide to do, I have found great value in learning to rest. God created the world in six days and on the seventh, He rested. This is a divine plan for worship, reflection and regeneration. The Sabbath time is to honor God's sovereignty and redemption. Not resting appropriately does not provide a release from pressures. When we are tired, our thinking isn't as sharp as it should be, and this makes us prone to the enemy's snares. Research suggests that when we are fatigued, it can affect our mood, memory, concentration, decision-making and emotional state.

This reminds me of the times when our daughter was a toddler. She would never admit to being tired or sleepy. Her brother would sometimes call her "Treasure Box" and she would smile and ask, "I'm Treasure Box, Matt? I'm Treasure Box." One Saturday evening, after a long day when she did not get a nap, he called her "my Treasure Box" and she went ballistic! Morgan started crying and shouting, "I'm not Treasure Box! That is not my name. Don't call me Treasure Box. Momma didn't name me Treasure Box!" We were stunned that she suddenly was repulsed at this term of endearment she earlier embraced. As her mother, I knew she was easily agitated because she was very tired. The point is that when Morgan was tired, she didn't hear Treasure Box in the same way she did when she was rested.

As adults, we are the same way. Research suggests that our emotions are negatively affected when we are tired or sleep deprived. A large body of research supports the connection between sleep deprivation and mood changes such as increased anger and aggression. The consensus seems to be that getting an adequate amount of sleep each night promotes improved mood and health.

Snare 8 – Lack of Time in God's Word

"This Book of the Law shall not depart from your mouth, but you shall meditate in it day and night, that you may observe to do according to all that is written in it. For then you will make your way prosperous, and then you will have good success."

~ Joshua 1:8 NKJV

I recently had a conversation about a situation brewing at a local church. As the young lady shared the details of the circumstances, I was able to discern her lack of knowledge of ministry protocol. Unbeknownst to her, she felt the music minister needed to "get in line" with the choir members. Later that evening, I reflected on the conversation and was saddened by this young lady's lack of knowledge of God's Word. Her ignorance caused her to support an attitude contrary to Scripture. God told Joshua to develop a lifestyle of studying God's Word (Jos 1:8). The discipline of study makes you keen in discerning God's will. It's easy to believe lies when you do not know the truth.

The people who have not exposed their hearts and minds to God's Word are susceptible to being offended without any conviction at all. Imagine yourself having lunch with two coworkers, one is saved and the other one isn't. You have committed to witnessing about Jesus Christ each time you have lunch together. It has also become common for you to gossip and criticize fellow members and leadership based on carnal and worldly thinking. What are the chances the unsaved coworker will receive your witness? This is what happens when we lack knowledge of the Lord and His Word. The less time we spend in God's Word, the less we can discern truth, which makes us very easy to snare.

Snare 9 - Picking Up Someone Else's Offense

> *"He who passes by and meddles in a quarrel not his own is like one who takes a dog by the ears."*
>
> ~ Proverbs 26:17 NKJV

Each person has his own problems. Sadly, some are willing to take on the offenses of someone else as if they were their own. This practice is irresponsible and immature. Accepting an offense as a sign of support or loyalty is a betrayal to self. Instead of joining in sin as a show of support, you should stand up for Christ. The unpopular and mature response is to pray and reaffirm God's Word. Rarely are all the circumstances, facts and truths known. When you willfully become offended on behalf of another, you are willingly declaring ought with your brother or sister without cause. When the alleged offender is guilty, it is still without cause to you since you are not the object of the offense.

The Proverbs writer suggests this meddling to be like grabbing a dog by the ears. If you know the nature of the beast, then grabbing a dog by the ears may quickly provoke a bite. This is an invitation to trouble and strife. Peter warns, *"But let none of you suffer as a murderer, a thief, an evildoer, or as a busybody in other people's matters"* (1Pe 4:15 NKJV).

There is safety traveling in your own lane. The attitude of joining in sin can have lasting repercussions. The fruit of offense is never spiritually profitable because it cultivates more sin and division.

Snare 10 – Out of Control

"Whoever has no rule over his own spirit Is like a city broken down, without walls."

~ Proverbs 25:28 NKJV

In ancient Palestine, walls enclosed a city for the purpose of safety. There were gates, which granted access and they were guarded day and night. If a known danger was approaching the gates, the city watchmen would alert citizens by sounding the alarm. This verse is speaking of the person who is unprotected, or vulnerable to attack, the one who is foolish. The out of control person is known to be short-sighted, argumentative, impulsive, irrational, and insensitive, instead of being watchful and prayerful. He is not in the safety of the city and too far away to hear the alarm. Being deficient in self-control is a reckless state. That person exposes himself to all sorts of danger – seen and unseen – because he is unprotected.

My mother used to quote lines of "Invictus" whenever she wanted to remind us to think rather than react: "It matters not how strait the gate, how charged with punishment the scroll; I am the master of my fate. I am the captain of my soul." In her own way, she was teaching us a lesson in self-control and sound thinking. We are stewards of our actions and should be led by the Holy Spirit and not the flesh.

Snare 11 – Improper Dependence

"For in Him we live and move and have our being, as also some of your own poets have said, 'for we are also His offspring."

~ Acts 17:28 NKJV

People often look to others to be their compass and comfort in life. While we are called to be relational, we are to place our faith in the Lord. It is in God that we find strength and refuge, not from other people. The development and establishment of relationships requires there to be some type of connection or bond. Relationships among friends, leaders and mentors often test one's independence because it becomes common to seek their advice or opinion on personal matters. You must have healthy boundaries. At no time should your dependency on others be above your relationship with the Lord. Neither should someone expect you to depend on them to be your source. In their proper position, few relationships are more valuable to you than those divinely ordained by God.

Our dependency must be in the One Who is divinely qualified: *"Trust in the LORD with all your heart and lean not on your own understanding; in all your ways submit to him, and he will make your paths straight"* (Prov 3:5-6 NIV). No matter the circumstances, we are to seek the Lord's wisdom before speaking to anyone. When the focus is upward, we are less vulnerable to being offended. The believers' hope is in the Lord, nowhere else. *"Great peace have those who love Your law, and nothing causes them to stumble"* (Ps 119:165 NKJV).

Snare 12 – Pride

"For I say, through the grace given to me, to everyone who is among you, not to think of himself more highly than he ought to think, but to think soberly, as God has dealt to each one a measure of faith."

~ Romans 12:3 NKJV

No one is immune to being offended. Many years ago, I was deeply offended by the actions of someone I loved deeply. In my struggle to trust the Lord to heal my heart, He whispered, "Do you think life can't happen to you like it happens to everyone else?" At that moment, I wanted to shake my fist at God. Instead, I wept and asked for forgiveness. Why? I was deeply offended because my pride told me that I was right, better than, and deserved better. I changed my prayer from Lord heal me to, "Lord, I thank you that you have given me the grace to walk this situation out in a way that brings glory to you." In a matter of days, the offense left me. Sometimes we become so enmeshed with ourselves that we do not consider what others are going through. As my soul was quieted, the offender was convicted, explained her situation, and asked for my forgiveness. If my pride had not gotten in the way earlier, I would have been able to discern her situation and not taken offense. Paul reminds us *"not to think of ourselves more highly than we ought to"* (Ro 12:3 NKJV). We must discern the Holy Spirit's conviction over flesh. (See Appendix E)

"The trap may be there, but it's your choice whether you stumble."
~ Margo W. Williams

Keep this in mind:

A snare/trap is strategically placed in a location that is common to the animal, but he is unable to see it. Once the animal steps into the trap he cannot free himself. Most traps are not designed to kill, instead they are to keep the animal from getting away. If the injured animal stays in the trap too long, the injury will cripple him, or he will suffer a slow death. To be freed, it requires a force greater and smarter than the animal to release it. In the animal's mind he wants to be free, but he does not know how to do it.

As believers, many don't want the pain of being offended and they have not discovered that they already possess the tools to be released. It is by the power of the Holy Spirit working within.

Ask yourself:

1. Which traps do I relate to? Why?

2. Identify and describe the temptations that have lured me into traps.
3. Explain how *"For in Him we live, and move, and have our being"* applies to avoiding the snares?

Pray

Father help me to see beyond how I feel today. Your Word is a lamp to my feet and a light to my path of life. As I study Your Word, help me to apply the truth to the circumstances of life. I receive Your instruction which leads to liberty. In Jesus' name. Amen.

Chapter 8
The Spirit of Offense

"And this I pray, that your love may abound still more and more in knowledge and all discernment, that you may approve the things that are excellent, that you may be sincere and without offense till the day of Christ."

~ Philippians 1:9-10 NKJV

One of the most fascinating aspects of our salvation is that the Holy Spirit comes in and takes residence in the heart of a believer at the moment of salvation. Psalm 139:7 teaches that there isn't any place we can go and be apart from God's Spirit since He is omnipresent. He is noted as the Helper and Teacher who leads us to truth. Knowing these attributes of God makes it difficult for us to believe that another type of spirit can oppress a born-again Christian. After all, we assume that the Holy Spirit's indwelling presence is all we need to ward off the forces of darkness. This is factual, but not true. As free-will agents, we have been given the right to make our own choices. Therefore, it is vital that we open ourselves to self-assessment to determine how we have contributed to our situations, whether they are good or bad.

Horses have keen peripheral vision, so they wear blinders to keep them from being distracted when racing or in public settings. When a person has received an offense, his inner harmony will be disturbed, which results in impaired vision. Like the horse, the offended person is unable to have a good view of what is behind, beside or in front of him. He has become so sensitive to what has occurred that he is unable to look beyond what appears to be the obvious. He becomes emotionally and spiritually distracted. He needs help in redirecting his focus.

The Apostle Paul told the Corinthians, *"While we do not look at the things which are seen, but at the things which are not seen. For the things which are seen are temporary, but the things which are not seen are eternal"* (2Cor 4:18 NKJV). The Corinthian believers were some of the most gifted and powerful Christians of that time, but they relished in their carnality. They allowed themselves to be led by their opinions and emotions rather than the Spirit of God. Also, the same holds true for the one oppressed by the Spirit of Offense; his mind, will and emotions are led by an evil spirit. This dark spirit works to convince the offended to walk in a super-sensitive state that creates retaliation and animosity. At this point, the offending spirit has blinded his vision.

Paul's desire was that the Philippians would have an abounding love for one another; grow in knowledge and be discerning. As we grow in our knowledge of the Lord, our perspective shifts. Jesus's desire is that we would mature into the fullness of His character, in every way. As He walked the earth, Jesus left an indisputable example for us to follow. If we are wise, we will come to accept the truth of knowing the Lord hasn't asked any of us to do as much as He required of His Son, so we ought to be eager to accept and adopt His ways. The Apostle Paul was a living example of the change God wants to see in each of us. At one time, he saw through the dark lens of the Law. After his Damascus Road conversion, his perspective for understanding changed in how he viewed the church. Earlier, Paul was violently passionate about his mistaken beliefs. The Lord orchestrated a divine confrontation, which served as the catalyst to change the trajectory of his life. Each time offense punches us in the gut, it has the power to negatively affect our daily walk. The sustained injuries may hinder us from standing and walking upright without a limp. In either case, the Lord does not want us to bear the pain of the injury. Certainly, this is not easy to do, but by all means it should be our desire.

When Jesus began to work miracles, He endured the snide remarks and whispers of village people questioning His authority because they knew Him as Mary and Joseph's son. Nothing was more offensive than being betrayed by Judas; one who walked with Him and shared ministry with Him. Scripture reminds us of the pain of being hurt by a friend, the one with whom we share our secrets. The beauty in Christ's offenses is how He chose to deal with them. We must remember that although He left Heaven to come to earth, Jesus walked the ground as a man. From His earthly birth, He experienced the same emotions we do today, yet He didn't give in to them. As Christians we know Jesus dealt with excruciating blows from the time of His arrival until His death, but they never took Him out of himself. Peter says that when Jesus was insulted and abused, He did not succumb to the offenses (1Pe 2:23). He chose not to retaliate.

Easily Offended

"The Lord will fight for you, and you have only to be silent."
~ Exodus 14:14 ESV

The prospect of being easily offended is very common in our society and church culture. Have you ever felt as if you had to "walk on eggshells" around certain people? Perhaps you have sat in silence so you would not disturb the peace in a group? I have experienced the agony of being a silent teammate for fear that my words would create offense. If you have ever had these experiences, then you were likely confronted with people who get offended easily. At one time in my life, I worked with a manager who seemed to relish in being offensive to others and ironically, he was easily offended. He would use his position to retaliate and avenge himself. What one thought was principle and honor, another saw it as under-developed emotions. After listening to his rage and performances, I would often wonder what really fueled his temperament. It is a certainty that anyone ignorant of their own strengths and weaknesses will surely find himself harmed by his own strength. That leader carried the Spirit of Offense wherever he went.

Being easily offended is often caused by ordinary, self-centered views of life. Whether he is a victim or not, he sees himself as a victim and he presumes that something is owed to him because he is offended. He makes a habit of complaining and being critical of others and situations. Many times, his complaints are an exercise in blame and finger pointing. He becomes devoted to building a case against his offender and he assumes the roles of attorney, judge and jury. Unfortunately, the easily offended is so engrossed in himself that he is barely able to appreciate the fullness of blessings in his own life. None of us are immune to this mindset and behavior. Being easily offended carries a thick wall of defense, so it is much easier to stay in that condition than to be delivered. After all, there is an emotionally charged pseudo-power that comes with the ability to gain illegitimate support.

"Past pains are carefully preserved within walls built around the heart."
~ Margo W. Williams

It is likely that the one who is easily offended is walking in the Spirit of Offense. Carrying offense is like wearing the same dirty and sweaty shirt every day believing you don't smell. Everyone around you can smell the odor, but rarely does anyone tell you. When they do, your reply is, "I don't smell anything. It's not me." If we're honest, then most people have some memories of being hurt or embarrassed by the words or actions of others, but we seldom take the time to investigate the source of the injury. Among the Body of Christ, many struggle with forgiveness, transparency, and trust. Each stemming from a wounded soul.

The Spirit of Offense is not a term you will find in the Bible, instead it is a spiritual principle connected to a stronghold, which is an incorrect way of thinking. This principle is usually illustrated as being an oppression or infirmity. A very clear picture of Satan's oppression is displayed with the woman who was bent over for 18 years. When Jesus was questioned about healing this woman on the Sabbath, He attributed her condition to the adversary. He responded, *"So ought not this woman, being a daughter of Abraham, whom Satan has bound—think of it—for eighteen years, be loosed from this bond on the Sabbath?"* (Lu 13:16 NKJV). It is important to look at what she could not do that she should have been able to do. Consider the length of time, the duration of the condition. Only when she encountered Jesus was she loosed from the infirmity.

We have been redeemed, but we must exercise our authority. This woman was dealing with a spirit that continually oppressed her, keeping her from standing upright and being able to see as she walked. I can imagine this woman's anguish. She was a daughter of God, went to the synagogue to worship and none of the spiritual leaders could help her. Daily she was reminded by her condition that she could not stand up, neither could she see ahead of her. Like this woman, the person who is easily offended is unable to free himself and is bound with a compromised posture, being unable to spiritually see, stand or walk upright.

Love Walk

> *"He has shown you, O man, what is good; And what does the LORD require of you but to do justly, to love mercy, and to walk humbly with your God?"*
>
> ~ Micah 6:8 NKJV

We are often challenged in our love walk because we do not recognize the essence of Godly love in our relationships. None of us were born to live a life without the fellowship of others. As we grow in relationships, it is inevitable that we will experience heartache, disappointments, rejection and betrayals. Only the naïve will believe that love does not hurt. It can and it will. It is not a matter of whether someone will hurt you, but more so an issue of how we respond to the offense. We are to have the approach of the Proverbs writer, he says, *"A friend loves at all times, and a brother is born for adversity"* (Prov 17:17 NKJV).

When unmet expectations are present, offense can creep in. It has been a long-standing observation that, "if you don't love, then you don't hurt." Only when there is a deep level of respect, love, and admiration for someone is there power to hurt, or offend. Literally, there is an inward acceptance that the other party matters, having significant value in your heart. When we sincerely value people or relationships, we care for them and make them priorities in our lives. That priority is often assumed to be reciprocated by the other party. It may be that the other party does not say or do what you expect of him, and disappointment enters. The disappointment clings to the mind, will and emotions, producing offense. If the offending party recognizes the ought and tries to correct the situation, then the offended will often verbalize the acceptance and keep the offense. This happens due to the inward hold: unforgiveness.

> *"A brother offended is harder to win than a strong city, and contentions are like the bars of a castle."*
>
> ~ Proverbs 18:19 NKJV

The root of offense is unforgiveness. Although forgiveness is a command, we must choose to be obedient. The Bible teaches that we are to forgive in the same way that Christ has forgiven us (Eph 4:32). For some, this seems like an impossible feat when we approach it in our own strength. For years, I've heard these remarks: "I just can't help it!" "I don't know if I can forgive him/her." "It's not right! I didn't deserve this." "I didn't do anything, they need to make it right, not me!" In the natural, each remark is a cry for divine help. In reality, there are some things we are unable to forgive without the help of the Holy Spirit. He is our empowering agent. He will do for us what we cannot do for ourselves.

To forgive, we must leave the high place and take the elevator to the basement. The lowest realm of our faith rests on the promise of God's love and forgiveness. There is nothing we can do to remove ourselves from the gracious love of the Lord. There were times in my life that this truth was the only place where I could find safety. We are loved despite ourselves, even when we were outside the covenant of salvation. Paul says, *"But God demonstrates His own love toward us, in that while we were still sinners, Christ died for us"* (Ro 5:8 NKJV). The love of God was proven with Christ's death, burial and resurrection. Just think: As filthy as we were, Jesus paid for our sins because of the Lord's unfailing, unyielding, steadfast, and enduring love. We all are recipients of this amazing grace. The person who withholds forgiveness is void of understanding the depth of his own depravity and lacks appreciation of the Lord's mercy. All too often when we are hurt by others, we judge ourselves against the offender. This is spiritual self-righteousness. Jeremiah made it clear, *"Let us search out and examine our ways, and turn back to the Lord"* (Lam 3:40 NKJV). None has reached perfection; therefore, we all stand to improve in our daily walk with the Lord.

Believers must remember that forgiveness does not make the offender right. Neither does unforgiveness make you justified in your pain. The act of forgiveness brings peace, liberty, and divine alignment into the soul of the offended. This takes faith in God and not in self, or the offender. You are literally saying, "Father, this is too hard for me to bear. I am giving you the offense. I am forgiving the offender, and everyone attached to it. I thank You that I have the mind of Christ and I ask You to help me think on what is lovely, true, pure, and admirable concerning the offender and the offense. By faith I accept that without You I can't do this, but by faith this is so." We stumble when we gauge forgiveness on how we feel. Every offense has been paid for with Jesus' blood. Forgiveness is a decision made according to faith in the finished work on the cross.

Faith functions by love. Are you trying to grow in love at the same rate you are trying to grow in faith?

Jesus Warns

"But He turned and said to Peter, "Get behind Me, Satan! You are an offense to Me, for you are not mindful of the things of God, but the things of men."

~ Matthew 16:23 NKJV

Since the time of Jesus, the religious leaders – Sadducees, Pharisees, Scribes – all became offended because of the truth. They were respected as experts in the Law, yet they failed in understanding what the Law meant. For this reason, the religious spirit was holding them hostage in the same way it captures believers today. Whenever we become rigid in our knowledge of something, we are prone to ignore the expanse of its practical meaning. Jesus said, *"And blessed is he who is not offended because of Me"* (Matt 11:6 NKJV). He came on the scene and challenged the spiritual authorities of the day. He did not sugarcoat or talk around the issues. Instead He confronted the lies and traditions they upheld. Jesus dared to preach words contrary to the teachings of the Sadducees and Pharisees.

I have imagined what it would have been like to sit in the synagogue listening to Jesus and hearing the under-breath comments, questioning His authority to speak. There are some today with the same audacity to question who is delivering God's Word because the preacher or teacher doesn't meet their trite standards. Be aware that Pharisees and Sadducees function today with new titles. The names have changed but the spirit is the same. They speak about things which they know nothing about. Their understanding is merely limited to words on the pages since it isn't understood in the spirit. They become offended because of their spiritual ignorance. This poses a great threat to the Body of Christ. We are called to teach according to the Word of God and not what we feel, think or reason. Poor Peter learned this valuable lesson when he told Jesus that the things He was saying about His death would not happen. Jesus quickly rebuked him and called him Satan (Matt 16:23). The point of

Jesus' sharp correction was to clear up any misunderstanding about truth. Peter meant well in what he was saying but it was contrary to the will of God. We do not get a "free pass" in handling God's Word.

This truth requires integrity of spiritual leaders. Jesus applauds those who recognize the truth and will stand for the truth over position, popularity, relationships, traditions, or social norms. He declared, *"And you shall know the truth, and the truth shall make you free"* (John 8:32 NKJV). Speaking the truth brings offense because it challenges the ignorant, blind, death, rebellious, and naïve to step over the snare and walk circumspectly toward the cross. Those who have set their affections on pleasing Christ find this to be easier than those who make a conscious decision to please themselves. *"Knowing this, that our old man was crucified with Him, that the body of sin might be done away with, that we should no longer be slaves of sin"* (Ro 6:6 NKJV). Crucifixion shows there has been a death, so we are to die to the thing that had the power to make us sin, even in our hearts.

The Spirit of Offense is clever in hindering us from receiving truth, healing, and deliverance from God. We must be aware of what is at work. The Spirit of Offense will rest upon us so that we are unable *"to take heed what you hear"* (Mk 4:24 NKJV). One of the most frustrating ills of the church is discerning how to deal with those who have been offended. In most faith circles, we know people who wander from church to church, unable to settle anywhere. They are caught between three malfunctioning realities. One, they are looking forward to a new faith community. Two, they are looking backward, making comparisons of where they came from. Three, they have unresolved conflict related to their first departure.

Certainly, there are various reasons to leave a church, which have nothing to do with offense. I am specifically addressing those who have left congregations out of an emotional annoyance. Jesus expected people to refuse His teachings when He said, *"And blessed is he who is not offended because of Me"* (Lk 7:23 NKJV). Isn't it like church people to get angry when they are confronted with their sin? People like to look at what is wrong with others and take cover – refuge – in private deception. The internal dial registers this thought: "What you don't know won't hurt you." Unfortunately, this kind of rhetoric is a failure of many to discern value. Believers must mature to the place wherein they are able to discern what is valuable versus what is worthless. Therefore, my response is, "What you don't deal with will deal with you!"

Testimony

Shortly after returning from our honeymoon, I received a call from a friend who wanted to "fill me in" on what she saw at our wedding. As I listened to her critical comments about a particular person, I became sad and disappointed. My disappointment was not with the one who was bearing the negative news, but the one she criticized. Later, when I spoke with the other friend, I questioned her about what I had been told and she became offended that I believed what was said. It was a matter of days, I regretted that I had opened myself to listen to the accusations about the other friend.

In time, as I was growing spiritually, the Holy Spirit addressed a few issues with me. First, He let me know that I had to accept responsibility for allowing the "news" to be shared with me. I had the choice to stop the talk, or to allow it to continue. Second, the conversation really had less to do with me and more with the one who brought the "news" to me. She was exposing her own heart. She had taken petty matters and interpreted them as significant and I was easy prey. Third, He prompted me to call the friend and apologize, asking her to forgive me for allowing someone else's words to come between us. By this time, I was able to clearly discern the Lord's voice and I knew what I was hearing was from the Lord. I recognized His promptings, but did not call my friend.

Many years passed and we didn't have any contact with one another. Sometime between the time of my parents' death, I became so convicted that I reached out to her, nearly 25 years later. We spoke over the phone, met and had a tearful reunion. The most difficult aspect of the entire event was lost time. Looking back, I can recall multiple times the Holy Spirit would bring her to my mind, I would pray for her and never made contact. Some of those times I would Google her name in hopes to "see where she was" but still I would not reach out. Why not? I was disappointed and ashamed that I had allowed someone else's words to influence how I felt about another friend, whom I sincerely loved.

Initially, when the "news" was told to me, I was hurt, but never angry. As I settled into married life, the hurt dissipated because all the "news" was petty. None of it really mattered; it was worthless. What made the difference is how I handled the "news" that was reported to me. I had walked in offense with myself. I knew better.

Ask yourself:

1. Identify and describe why I am easily offended by certain people and situations. Specifically, what is it that really bothers me about them?
2. Based on how I feel about those people, explain how my faith in God is increased.
3. Describe how I plan to stand for truth in dealing with those with whom I am easily offended.

Pray

Father, I do not want to carry the Spirit of Offense, neither do I want to dishonor You. Help me to minister healing to myself. As I am being healed, I am able to see other people through Your eyes. In Jesus' name. Amen.

Part Three
The CHANGE

"What God has purposed for you is too big for you to be petty."

~Margo W. Williams

How Do You Change?

"Therefore, if anyone is in Christ, he is a new creation; old things have passed away; behold, all things have become new."
~ 2Corinthians 5:17 NKJV

Change is an unavoidable participant in life. Whether it is recognized internally or externally, nothing stays the same except for the Word of God. From the moment of salvation, the believer becomes a new creature in Christ. While he is someone different, it takes time for him to learn the integral aspects of transformation. You can compare this change to the birth of a baby. Instinctively, the baby doesn't have to be taught how to cry and eat. However, as he grows, he must be taught to walk, use the bathroom and talk. Otherwise, he will continue to behave as a baby. The teachings involve love, instruction, correction and modeling. As that child grows, the good parent will coach him through his doubts and fears. The new believer must also be taught the new way of life. He will experience the friction between the old and the new self, the unrighteous and the righteous. The Holy Spirit will coach him through conviction.

Before Israel was released from Babylonian captivity the Lord encouraged them about what was ahead. He said, *"Do not remember the former things, nor consider the things of old"* (Is 43:18 NKJV). In essence, they were told to focus on what will be different, what is changing, and it was going to be greater than what they had known from the past. He went on to tell them that He would be with them under all circumstances and conditions they will face. For us, God is telling us that we are to forget the life we lived before Christ. Whatever were the beliefs, attitudes and behaviors before salvation, our mind has now changed, and the old ways are no longer sufficient.

For the believer, change is proportional to the will. God has given man the right to choose how he lives. With this right, he also assumes the consequences of his choices. Both the offender and the offended are responsible for responding to offenses in ways that bring glory to God. If we claim the name of Christ, we are to intentionally exchange old ways for the new ways. When John the Baptist was preparing for the appearance of Jesus' ministry, he was confronted with the hypocritical religious leaders of his day. They showed up, but had no desire to repent and be baptized. He challenged their presence by telling them to *"produce fruit in keeping with repentance"* (Lk 3:8 NIV). Isn't that what God is requiring of us today? If we have sincerely turned from our old ways and confessed faith in Christ, then we are to live a lifestyle that reflects repentance. The fruit of our lives should bring pleasure to God. Change can be difficult, but in Christ we are able to do all things well. This is when we ask the Holy Spirit to help us change.

Chapter 9
Reconciliation

"Now all things are of God, who has reconciled us to Himself through Jesus Christ, and has given us the ministry of reconciliation."

~ 2Corinthians 5:18 NKJV

Reconciliation is an accounting process designed to resolve discrepancies between what has been claimed and what occurred. The purpose is to reconcile or ensure there is agreement between two accounts. The biblical principle of reconciliation is the same, to settle differences between people with the goal of being able to walk together in harmony again. The Lord's provision for harmony was purchased with Jesus' blood at Calvary. According to Paul, not only did God buy us back from Satan, He balanced our ledgers. Whatever we have done has been paid in full, no longer being charged to our accounts (2Cor 5:19). As Christ's ambassadors, His official representatives on the earth, we are assigned to embody the responsibility and privilege of being agents of reconciliation.

Reconcile
"re" - prefix
- To restore to friendship or harmony
- To make consistent or congruous
Merriam-Webster Dictionary

People doubt whether true reconciliation is possible. Many have written books on forgiveness and reconciliation, yet we are prone to ignore or reject the idea of coming together after an offense. The Bible is clear that forgiveness between believers is the Lord's expectation. In the Book of Matthew, Jesus told the story of a servant who had a large debt he was unable to pay. He stood to lose his family and all his belongings. Knowing the gravity of his situation he fell on his knees and asked for mercy. This act of humility led his master to release him from the debt. The Bible describes the master as being *"moved with compassion"* (Matt 18:26).

> *"Bearing with one another, and forgiving one another, if anyone has a complaint against another; even as Christ forgave you, so you also must do."*
>
> ~ Colossians 3:13 NKJV

Sadly, the same servant left the master, found one of his colleagues that owed him a fraction of what he had owed the master, and he refused to forgive his debt. In case you may be comparing your personal situation to this example and justifying your decision to withhold forgiveness, the story does not end there. His behavior caused such a stir that his fellow servants went to their master and reported his shameful actions. This servant was so absorbed in himself that he didn't notice he was being watched. Upon learning what happened, the master became angry and changed his mind. He rescinded the acquittal and sentenced the wicked servant to be tortured in prison until his debt was repaid. *"So, my heavenly Father also will do to you if each of you, from his heart, does not forgive his brother his trespasses"* (Matt 18:35 NKJV). The principle is not whether someone admits to their wrong, it is about recognizing what God has done for you. As members of the Body of Christ, we really have a divine obligation to forgive others, whether they apologize or not. This is where many get trapped.

The next step is reconciliation, which is God's method of relational restoration. To be reconciled, we must first forgive, or "let go" of the offense. When there has been an offense, the offender should repent of his actions. This is interesting because James counsels, *"Confess your faults one to another, and pray one for another, that ye may be healed"* (Ja 5:16 NKJV). The act of repenting, or confessing our faults is ingenious. I believe true restoration is only possible when each party acknowledges his individual contributions. This is not a time to weigh the scales, but a time to empty the bag. Remember, God knows every man's heart, and His blood covers all stains. There are some offenses that even the best of us are challenged with reconciling, so we must be diligent to pray for the barrier to be destroyed. Keep in mind that forgiveness is an individual choice, but reconciliation involves agreement of at least two parties.

The adage "forgive and forget" presumes that we are to forgive and forget what has happened. This saying has been repeated as counsel in reconciling relationships between loved ones, but it is an example of poor scriptural interpretation. First, forgiveness is an unconditional command, which is not tied to forgetting. The Greek word for forgive is *"aphiemi,"* which means to release or let go of a debt.[19] The Ephesian record says, *"And be kind to one another, tenderhearted, forgiving one another, even as God in Christ forgave you"* (Eph 4:32 NKJV). We, as Christ followers, have been given the extraordinary gift of mercy and grace and it is purely based on God's love and nothing we have done. Second, forgetting is peculiar in that the Bible teaches that God forgives and forgets (Is 43:25). This means that He does not hold the sins, or offenses, against us once He has forgiven. In Philippians 3:13-14, Paul instructs us to *"forget what lies behind and strain forward to what lies ahead,"* which is consistent in meaning. Paul doesn't forget, instead he chooses not to focus on what is in the past. Neither should we.

> *"When we allow God's love to trump our anger, we are able to experience restoration in relationships."*
> ~ Gwen Smith[20]

---

[19] https://www.blueletterbible.org/lang/lexicon/lexicon.cfm?t=kjv&strongs=g863
[20] https://gwensmith.net/when-love-trumps-anger/

This is often easier said than done. Our brain has a depository system, which houses the stories of our lives, especially those which affect our souls. When trust has been broken, it may take an extended period to process through to regain trust. Even if trust has been re-established, the relationship may never be restored. There must be an awareness that some broken relationships are the consequence of sin. If this is the case, reconciliation is still possible. If one party resists or rejects, the willing party can reconcile within himself. This can be done by exercising the honor and privilege of interceding for God's will to be done and to have peace. Peace is a by-product of being in right-standing with the Lord. It cannot be manufactured or imitated. Although Jesus is the Prince of Peace, we must be willing to receive what He offers. After attacking Job's character, his friend Eliphaz offered a profound word of counsel, *"Now acquaint yourself with Him, and be at peace; thereby good will come to you"* (Job 22:21 NKJV). It is only by choosing to live by God's principles are we granted peace.

As free-will agents, we have the authority to pray with the expectation that what we request will happen, by faith according to God's will. In sincere and diligent prayer, God changes the one who prays first. If you have been serving the Lord for some time, you recognize that most prayers, which involve another person's heart, takes time to come to pass. God does His best work when the odds appear to be stacked against us and we feel lonely. It is these times that we garner the strength to go deeper in the Lord. As intimacy increases with God, we gain more insight into who we really are. Herein we accept what has happened, the effect it has on us and the lessons learned. This is reconciliation in its purest form.

Spiritual Identity

"And that you put on the new man which was created according to God, in true righteousness and holiness."

~ Ephesians 4:24 NKJV

A few weeks ago, I spoke with a family member whom I have never met before. The phone call was prompted because of reading his social media posting. He had been offended by how he felt he was treated after revealing his identity to another family member. The conversation was consistent and insightful as he spoke about our family heritage. His vernacular was filled with the mutual language of love, respect, honor and pride concerning who we are as a family. Under the most unusual circumstances, we felt a deep sense of family unity although our paths had never physically crossed. Instinctively, we both knew who we were as descendants of the same great-grandfather. Shortly after the call the newfound cousin shared photos, which held a strong resemblance to others in the family. There was something that carried or existed in the genes of our descendants which was unique to being produced from the same tree. Our DNA defined us as cousins.

As Christians, our natural heritage was determined before the foundation of the earth, but our spiritual identity was born at Calvary. God, our Father, is self-existing, having no beginning or end. In Himself, He is eternal. The Bible says, *"In the beginning God created the Heavens and the earth"* (Gen 1:1 NKJV). Everything we know about the physical and material aspects of life came into existence out of God's creation. He told Jeremiah, *"Before I formed you in the womb, I knew you, and before you were born I set you apart, I appointed you as a prophet to the nations"* (Jer 1:5 NKJV). There was a purpose for Jeremiah's life prior to his birth, and there is a purpose for each of our lives also. Although this text refers to Jeremiah's calling, further Scriptures confirm our spiritual existence before our birth. Once we come into the earth our identities are influenced by genetics, family, culture, and values.

> *"Therefore, if anyone is in Christ, he is a new creation; old things have passed away; behold, all things have become new."*
> ~ 2Corinthians 5:17 NKJV

When we are born again, we take on a new nature, which demands that our identity be found in Christ. This means that the center of the old nature was self, but the center of the new self is Christ. Outside appearance is not a good indicator to verify identity. According to Webster, by definition, identity is the distinguishing character personality of an individual, or the condition of being the same with something described or asserted. Therefore, a person's identity is what separates one person from another: a measurable difference. Herein is where we home in on personality, value and beliefs. These are areas easily ignored because they aren't always noticeable. For example, it's possible to be a part of an affluent family, which is known for their philanthropy, but that doesn't mean you have the means or desire to help others. You have your own identity.

When investigators try to solve a crime, one of the first things they do is secure the area to canvas for evidence. Various items are examined to determine the identity of potential parties involved in the crime. If hair is found, the investigators will conduct a hair analysis to obtain the race and ethnicity of the potential suspect. Unfortunately, there are millions of people belonging to the same race, each having a different DNA. However, if fingerprints and blood are left on the scene, the investigators have a greater chance of finding the offender. The Bible teaches that life is in the blood of man (Lev 17:11). While every organ in the body needs blood to function, each person's blood has enzymes which are unique to that individual. The blood reveals the race, sex, hair color, eye color, and medical conditions, but it cannot tell you who someone is until there is a match. The case will remain unsolved until there is a person to match the identity credentials. As believers, the evidence of our identity is found in our salvation, re-birth credentials.

Re-Birth Credentials

"Flesh gives birth to flesh, but Spirit gives birth to spirit."
~ John 3:15 ESV

In Ephesians 1:3-14, Paul masterfully unpacks who we are as Christ-followers. Despite his circumstances of being in prison, he paints a powerful picture of Christian identity. Before gaining entrance into a foreign country, you must show proof of citizenship. The passport is a universal tool issued by all countries on the globe to verify the identity and nationality of the holder.[21] Immigration officers are aware that each traveler had to furnish credentials, such as a birth certificate and social security card, to prove identity prior to being issued the official passport. As Christians, God spiritually credentials us. Ephesians tells us that we are chosen, included in Christ, sealed by the Holy Spirit, and given gifts by God.

Credential 1 - Chosen by God

> *"Just as He **chose us in Him** before the foundation of the world, that **we should be holy and without blame** before Him in love, having predestined us to **adoption** as sons by Jesus Christ to Himself, according to the good pleasure of His will."*
>
> ~ Ephesians 1:4-5 NKJV

God had already chosen us before the world came into existence. This is an incredible thought. We did not choose Him; he had already chosen us. We had to accept Him. Before we were born, God purposed that we would live for Him. This is an act of grace; therefore, we are unable to take any credit for finding Christ. We were already accepted. We are adopted.

Credential 2 - Included in Christ

> *"**In Him you also trusted**, after you heard the word of truth, the gospel of your salvation; in whom also, having believed, you were sealed with the Holy Spirit of promise."*
>
> ~ Ephesians 1:13 NKJV

---

[21] https://www.passportindex.org/passport.php

Society wants us to believe that our identity is found in what we do and what we have, but it is found in Christ alone. Who we are, is in what God through Christ, has provided. In this text, Paul declares to the Ephesians that everything the Jews have in God, they have it also. In Christ, there isn't any favoritism.

Credential 3 - Sealed with the Holy Spirit

*"In Him you also trusted, after you heard the word of truth, the gospel of your salvation; in whom also, having believed, you were **sealed with the Holy Spirit** of promise, who is the guarantee of our inheritance until the redemption of the purchased possession, to the praise of His glory."*

~ Ephesians 1:13-14 NKJV

When you apply for college, the admissions department will request an official copy of your transcript. This copy is stamped as being official or sealed, meaning that an authorized official of the school verified the transcript and mailed it. Therefore, a seal is a sign of ownership. The Holy Spirit's seal carries the assurance that we are securely owned and that we are official. We are sealed until Jesus returns.

Credential 4 - Given Gifts by God

*"In Him we have **redemption** through His blood, the forgiveness of sins, according to the riches of His grace."*

~ Ephesians 1:7 NKJV

Who we are in Christ is an act of the grace of God. With Jesus' blood He bought our redemption and forgave our sins – past, present and future. Jesus paid the price for us to be set free from the penalty and the power of sin. We cannot earn it. It's a gift called grace.

Who we are as believers is found in these genetic credentials of salvation. Positionally, by walking in offense we are either denying our true identity or revealing our lack of knowledge. The first step to overcoming soul wounds is to know who we are. Then we can firmly stand. Unlike a physical wound, the soul has a way of impairing our sight. It is difficult to clearly recognize truth when the mind, emotions and will are out of balance, or infected. Offenses often act as a re-injury to a pre-existing wound. Therefore, what we are designed to become and do, is often delayed or lost in living with an unhealed soul.

We are to see ourselves as God sees us. Colossians 3:2-3 says, *"Set your mind on things above, not on things on the earth. For you died, and your life is hidden with Christ in God"* (NKJV). There must be an intentional decision to let go of the old image of self. Rather than accepting feelings of worry, doubt, insecurity, and rejection, we are to exchange those emotions with truth. It is in knowing Christ that we discover who we are. The shed blood of Jesus paid for our redemption, declaring the believer to be righteous. This right-standing confirms our identity and provides access to certain rights and privileges.

Rights and Privileges

"Blessed be the God and Father of our Lord Jesus Christ, who has blessed us with every spiritual blessing in the heavenly places in Christ."

~ Ephesians 1:3 NKJV

Live in Freedom

"Stand fast therefore in the liberty by which Christ has made us free, and do not be entangled again with a yoke of bondage."

~ Galatians 5:1 NKJV

We are sons and daughters of God, not slaves. We are no longer bound to any sin. We are forgiven. We live by faith in the finished work on the cross.

Maintain Peace

> *"The Lord will bless His people with peace."*
> ~ Psalm 29:11 NKJV

Peace is a state of being and is sourced from God. The Hebrew word *"shalom,"* means "completeness, wholeness, wealth, health, and rest." Peace is a by-product of having an intimate relationship with God and knowing His Word.

Be Fearless

> *"For you did not receive the spirit of bondage again to fear, but you received the Spirit of adoption by whom we cry out, "Abba, Father."*
> ~ Romans 8:15 NKJV

The Bible says that fear is a spirit that does not come from God. We have been given love, power and soundness of mind (2Tim 1:7).

Victory

> *"Now thanks be to God who always leads us in triumph in Christ, and through us diffuses the fragrance of His knowledge in every place."*
> ~ 2Corinthians 2:14 NKJV

We will have trials, but victory belongs to us.

Power of Attorney

> *"And these signs will follow those who believe: in My name they will cast out demons; they will speak with new tongues; they will take up serpents; and if they drink anything deadly,*

it will by no means hurt them; they will lay hands on the sick, and they will recover."

~ Mark 16:17-18 NKJV

The covenant of salvation gives the believer authority to pray and operate in Jesus' name.

Abundance

"But seek first the Kingdom of God and His righteousness, and all these things shall be added to you."

Matthew 6:33 NKJV

It is not God's will that we lack in any area of life. He has already given us everything we need; we are to reach for it and steward over what we have.

God Says

I Am…

His child – John 1:12
Fearfully and wonderfully made – Psalm 139:14
God's Masterpiece – Ephesians 2:10
I am to God the fragrance of Christ among those who are being saved and those who are perishing – 2Corinthians 2:15
An ambassador for Christ – 2Corinthians 5:20
Chosen – Ephesians 1:4
A son of light and not of darkness – 1Thessalonians 5:5
A doer of the Word and blessed in my actions – James 1:22, 25

I have…

A living hope – 1Peter 1:3
The mind of Christ – 1Corinthians 2:16

Peace with God – Romans 5:1
An anchor to my soul – Hebrews 6:19
The tongue of the learned – Isaiah 50:4
Put off the old man and have put on the new man, which is renewed in knowledge, after the image of Him Who created me – Colossians 3:9-10
Been raised up with Christ and seated in heavenly places – Ephesians 2:6

I have been…
Redeemed by the Blood of Jesus – Revelation 5:9
Set free from Satan's control – Colossians 1:13
Predestined to be like Jesus – Ephesians 1:11
Given a sound mind – 2Timothy 1:7
Given the Holy Spirit – 2Corinthians 1:22
Given all things pertaining to life and godliness – 2Peter 1:3
Access to God – Ephesians 3:12
I have been given exceedingly great and precious promises by God by which I am a partaker of God's divine nature – 2Peter 1:4

I can…
Do all things through Christ – Philippians 4:13
Come to come boldly before the throne of God to find mercy and grace in my time of need – Hebrews 4:16
Quench the fiery darts – Ephesians 6:16
Declare liberty to those who are captive – Isaiah 61:1
Defeat the enemy – Revelation 12:11

I cannot…
Be separated from God's love – Romans 8:35-39
Be removed from God's hand – John 10:29
Be condemned – 1Corinthians 11:32

Since I have died, I no longer live for myself, but for Christ – 2Corinthians 5:14-15

We must know who we are in Christ. This knowledge has nothing to do with emotions and everything to do with living in the authority of our salvation. What someone has done to you and how you feel about it does not change who and what God says that you are. Who you really are is defined by your re-birth. (See Appendix D)

"Your identity is not in who you think you are but who God says you are."
~ Margo Williams

Ask yourself:

1. What relationships exist in my life that I need to reconcile?
2. Identify and describe what stands in the way of me taking the first step to reconciliation.
3. If I decided to reconcile, how will my life be more enriched?

Pray

Father, because of my salvation I am a new creature in Christ. The things I used to do no longer match who I am today. When I forget the new way of living, please gently remind me that You have made all things new in me. In Jesus' name. Amen.

Chapter 10
Maturity

"But the fruit of the Spirit is love, joy, peace, longsuffering, kindness, goodness, faithfulness, gentleness, self-control. Against such, there is no law."

~ Galatians 5:22-23 NKJV

It is common for Christians to label themselves as being mature while demonstrating immature ways. Behavior is the essence of what is rooted in the belief system. As we journey through the days of our lives, we have thoughts we cherish. The appreciation for these thoughts may go back as far as childhood. Without much thought, early beliefs become the GPS for how we make choices. They direct our actions and reactions to life's good times and bad, to provide our platform and protection. For many, our beliefs are passed down through our birth families. Within this unit, each of us develop an understanding of who we are.

Each family has a unique mode of communication, a way they process emotions, and enforce discipline. Sociologists and psychologists suggest that we develop a sense of self from the context of our family of origin. For example, if you grow up surrounded by love, encouragement, and security, it's a good sign you will have a positive sense of who you are. On the contrary, growing up in chaos, abuse, and negativity may result in a poor self-image. The picture you capture of yourself reflects what you have learned to believe about yourself. There are many riddles and rhymes children chant to build confidence and esteem, but they seldom succeed in an environment that isn't consistent and conducive to growth. As a child my mother used to recite the words of a poem called "Children Learn What They Live," by Dr. Dorothy Law Nolte.

An excerpt:

"If children live with criticism, they learn to condemn.
If children live with hostility, they learn to fight.
If children live with fear, they learn to be apprehensive.
If children live with pity, they learn to feel sorry for themselves.
If children live with ridicule, they learn to feel shy.
If children live with jealousy, they learn to feel envy.
If children live with shame, they learn to feel guilty.
If children live with encouragement, they learn confidence."[22]

In either circumstance, the self-image is not questioned until it is faced with those who challenge its validity. These beliefs bleed into our spiritual belief system. The writer of Romans says, *"Be not conformed to this world: be ye transformed by the renewing of your mind, that ye may prove what is that good, and acceptable, and perfect will of God"* (Ro 12:2 NKJV). According to Strong's, the Greek word for conform is *"syschēmatizō"* (soos-khay-mat-id'-zo), which means to mold or shape one's behavior to the example or standard of another.[23] The illustration is compared to squeezing or forcing oneself into a mold. Herein, the world's values and patterns are not conducive to the believer. God does not force anything on us. He graciously offers us the choice to change. In choosing to follow God, we are making the decision to allow the Holy Spirit to rule in our hearts. When people are forced to agree, accept, or conform, it produces deficiency in spiritual growth. We are to be changed. By contrast, the Greek word *"metamorphóō"* (met-am-or-fo'-o), means to be transformed.[24] This is the same word used to describe the process of a caterpillar turning into a butterfly. Once a butterfly emerges, the form of the caterpillar

---

[22] http://www.empowermentresources.com/info2/childrenlearn-long_version.html
[23] "G4964 - *syschēmatizō* - Strong's Greek Lexicon (KJV)." Blue Letter Bible. Accessed 5 Sep, 2019. https://www.blueletterbible.org/lang/lexicon/lexicon.cfm?Strongs=G4964&t=KJV
[24] https://www.blueletterbible.org/lang/lexicon/lexicon.cfm?ot=NASB&strongs=g3339&t=kjv#lexSearch

has been eliminated. If you weren't aware of the life cycle of the egg, caterpillar, chrysalis and butterfly, then you couldn't imagine something so delicate and intricately beautiful would have been produced from a worm. From the inside out, the caterpillar becomes a butterfly. Likewise, we are to be changed from the person we used to be as we come into the knowledge of God's Word. If we allow the Word to wash and dwell within our hearts our beliefs change.

Keep in mind that we are a triune being, encompassed with spirit, soul and body, formed in the image of God the Father, Jesus the Son, and Holy Spirit. Jesus, who is God, came and walked the earth in human form. Jesus, our Redeemer is our Mediator, Brother and compassionate High Priest. The writer of Hebrews says, *"For we do not have a High Priest who cannot sympathize with our weaknesses, but was in all points tempted as we are, yet without sin"* (Heb 4:15 NKJV). Jesus has felt what we feel and is compassionate towards us as He knows and understands our feelings and emotions. We are not to pretend that our feelings don't exist, but we are to be good stewards of them. While sociologists and psychologists have spent years studying how to control negative emotions, all the theories and practices seem to wane in effectiveness without humble submission to the power of the Holy Spirit. As we grow in our knowledge of the Lord, the coaching of the Holy Spirit produces the Fruit of the Spirit.

"Fruit is always the miraculous, the created; it is never the result of willing, but always a growth. The fruit of the Spirit is a gift of God, and only He can produce it. They who bear it know as little about it as the tree knows of its fruit. They know only the power of Him on whom their life depends"
~ Dietrich Bonhoeffer
The Cost of Discipleship

One of the best ways to determine how well we are maturing in our emotions, is to face adversity. The absence of tension provides a false reading. It is very easy to appear loving, patient, kind, and self-controlled when we aren't confronted with what we don't like. Too often believers will resort to their unsaved default when feelings become bruised and emotions are inflated. This is one of the most difficult areas of our lives to regulate. Our feelings are often a response to fluctuating circumstances. The good news is that we have the indwelling presence of the Holy Spirit who will teach, guide and convict us of sin. Every time we yield ourselves to Him, God has a way of strengthening our souls – mind, will and emotions.

"You are only as mature as your most immature fruit."
~ Pastor J.D. Greear

Our spiritual growth moves us from being ignorant and childish to being wise and mature, exercising self-control. Scripture reveals that Jesus' emotions ranged from joy to agony, but He never yielded to sin. He lived in a state of joy regardless of his circumstances, He said, *"These things I have spoken to you, that My joy may remain in you, and that your joy may be full"* (John 15:11 NKJV). Our joy is found in having a faith-filled, experiential knowledge of Him. We are to intimately know the Lord, having individual testimonies of His working in our lives. When we can reference a personal history with the Lord, we are less likely to doubt or be easily shaken. The part that really touches my heart is what Jesus says prior to going to the cross. Being profoundly aware of his pending death, He says, *"Father, if it is Your will, take this cup away from Me; nevertheless, not My will, but Yours, be done"* (Lk 22:42 NKJV). Jesus, in His humanity, recognized that it is all about God's will being done in Him, not His personal preference. We see Him broken and resolute: Not wanting to die, but surrendering to God's will for His life. We can do the same. God's will is far greater than our own. He is all knowing, all wise, and all loving. When we begin to follow Christ's example, it will feel difficult. In time, the closer we follow Jesus, the easier it becomes to agree with His way.

I have discovered that spiritual maturity is a choice. We must be intentional to posture ourselves to grow and mature in the Lord.

The Apostle Paul repeatedly referred to the immature believers of his day. He associated their behaviors with children. The Hebrews writer suggests that the believer is expected to grow up. He says, *"For though by this time you ought to be teachers, you need someone to teach you again the first principles of the oracles of God; and you have come to need milk and not solid food"* (Heb 5:12 NKJV). The closer we are to the Lord, the more our character is to reflect His nature. Peter reminds the church that knowledge alone is not a measure of Christian maturity. He says we are to grow in *"knowledge and grace"* (2Pe 3:18). We gain spiritual stamina and strength when we properly apply what has been taught and read. Knowledge alone is not power.

    This lack of maturity is a great barrier to reconciliation. As believers, we cannot accept spiritual immaturity to be the norm for us. Immaturity directly affects the body of Christ. Although no one can boast of being perfect in God, we are to live our lives in a way that honors Him. We are to awaken daily with the commitment to choose the Lord's way over our own. Paul admonishes the believer to give his entire being to God (Ro 12:1). When living is submitted to God, the natural man begins to mature. In a sense a spontaneous, organic change called sanctification occurs in the soul. The believer who is being sanctified is "setting himself apart" with the ultimate goal of "returning to his proper state."

> *"Things are sanctified when they are used for the purpose God intends."*
> ~ Baker Evangelical Dictionary of Biblical Theology[25]

In a religious sense, many have equated sanctification as outward displays of performance, relationships and presence. On the surface, this seems to be correct, but sanctification is a much deeper work. Jesus said, *"Sanctify them by the truth; your word is truth"* (John 17:17 NKJV). It is impossible for the Word of God to separate you unless you are disciplined to study and meditate. Herein is how the Holy Spirit can sanctify your life. This is like peeling away the layers of an

---

[25] https://www.biblestudytools.com/dictionaries/bakers-evangelical-dictionary/sanctification.html

onion. Picture yourself preparing a recipe that requires an onion to be cut, layer by layer. With each slice is a release of a powerful gas that makes you cry. Not one time do you consider omitting the onion because it adds a rich flavor. The process of sanctification cuts away the old habits, thoughts and desires, one at a time. Removing the old can be painful, so the Lord extends this process throughout the life of the believer. Sanctification is designed to change you; therefore, it can be painful.

This course will require you to make adjustments in your life. You become intensely aware of how you respond to others. When you are offended, the sanctification process acts as a testing ground. At this point you declare, "Lord, not my will, but Yours be done in me." Just like the onion has a distinctive aroma and power, so does your life. A surrendered life to Christ carries the fragrance of the Spirit: *"For we are to God the fragrance of Christ among those who are being saved and among those who are perishing"* (2Cor 2:15 NKJV). The Lord is pleased when we forsake what is common for what is righteous. The sanctification process has the power to offend the enemy's schemes, or *"escape the trap of the devil"* (2Tim 2:26). Here is where you can have a clearer picture of offense. Rather than seeing an offense as something to receive, you recognize it for what it is. It is a trap. The more sanctified you are, the easier it is to allow the Lord to work in you, through you and for you. Although the offensive action may be painful, you choose to refrain from responding with petty behaviors.

To go through a process of sanctification, there must be an intentional and daily submission to God. This submission is God's will and is provoked by the Holy Spirit. When we discern that He is moving on us to change, we are to obey. Paul asserts that we ought to refrain from *"grieving the Holy Spirit of God" (Eph 4:30)*. Anytime the believer hears His voice and resists, he is in danger as it is a form of rebellion. We also recognize that the Bible teaches that those who are led by God's spirit are known as His children (Ro 8:14).

A sanctified, mature believer refuses to allow offense to alter his position. Know that God has *"raised us up together and made us sit together in the heavenly places in Christ Jesus"* (Eph 2:6). In essence, the higher you are in Christ the clearer your vision becomes. A mature and sanctified life will empower you to *"consider how we may spur one another on toward love and good deeds"* despite offense (Heb 10:24). There is a definite link between sanctification and spiritual maturity. If we are sincere in serving the Lord, we won't allow ourselves to remain unchanged.

Characteristics of Spiritual Immaturity

"Examine yourselves as to whether you are in the faith. Test yourselves. Do you not know yourselves, that Jesus Christ is in you?—unless indeed you are disqualified."

~ 2Corinthians 13:5 NKJV

Prideful

"Do you see a man wise in his own eyes? There is more hope for a fool than for him."

~ Proverbs 26:12 NKJV

Hard to get along with others

"For I fear lest, when I come, I shall not find you such as I wish, and that I shall be found by you such as you do not wish; lest there be contentions, jealousies, outbursts of wrath, selfish ambitions, backbiting, whispering, conceits and tumults."

~ 2Corinthians 12:20 NKJV

Unable to feed self

"And I, brethren, could not speak to you as to spiritual people but as to carnal, as to babes in Christ. I fed you with milk and not with solid food; for until now you were not able to receive it, and even now you are still not able; for you are

still carnal. For where there are envy, strife, and divisions among you, are you not carnal and behaving like mere men? For when one says, "I am of Paul," and another, "I am of Apollos," are you not carnal?"

~ 1Corinthians 3:1-4 NKJV

Easily Offended

"For there is not a just man on earth who does good and does not sin. Also do not take to heart everything people say, lest you hear your servant cursing you."

~ Ecclesiastes 7:20-21 NKJV

Selfish

"I say then: Walk in the Spirit, and you shall not fulfill the lust of the flesh. For the flesh lusts against the Spirit, and the Spirit against the flesh; and these are contrary to one another, so that you do not do the things that you wish."

~ Galatians 5:16-17 NKJV

Won't listen

"For everyone who partakes only of milk is unskilled in the word of righteousness, for he is a babe. But solid food belongs to those who are of full age, that is, those who by reason of use have their senses exercised to discern both good and evil."

~ Hebrews 5:13-14 NKJV

Reject wisdom

"Till we all come to the unity of the faith and of the knowledge of the Son of God, to a perfect man, to the measure of the stature of the fullness of Christ; that we should no longer be children, tossed to and fro and carried about with every wind

of doctrine, by the trickery of men, in the cunning craftiness of deceitful plotting."

~ Ephesians 4:13-14 NKJV

Childish thinking

"Brethren, do not be children in understanding; however, in malice be babes, but in understanding be mature."

~ 1Corinthians 14:20 NKJV

Confusion and Evil

"But if you have bitter envy and self-seeking in your hearts, do not boast and lie against the truth. This wisdom does not descend from above, but is earthly, sensual, demonic. For where envy and self-seeking exist, confusion and every evil thing are there."

~ James 3:14-16 NKJV

Qualities of the Spiritually Mature

"I beseech you therefore, brethren, by the mercies of God, that you present your bodies a living sacrifice, holy, acceptable to God, which is your reasonable service. And do not be conformed to this world, but be transformed by the renewing of your mind, that you may prove what is that good and acceptable and perfect will of God."

~ Romans 12:1-2 NKJV

Disciplined in Study of the Word

> *"But solid food belongs to those who are of full age, that is, those who by reason of use have their senses exercised to discern both good and evil."*
>
> ~ Hebrews 5:14 NKJV

Sound Thinking

> *"Finally, brethren, whatever things are true, whatever things are noble, whatever things are just, whatever things are pure, whatever things are lovely, whatever things are of good report, if there is any virtue and if there is anything praiseworthy—meditate on these things."*
>
> ~ Philippians 4:8 NKJV

Knowledgeable and Productive

> *"But also, for this very reason, giving all diligence, add to your faith virtue, to virtue knowledge, to knowledge self-control, to self-control perseverance, to perseverance godliness, to godliness brotherly kindness, and to brotherly kindness love. For if these things are yours and abound, you will be neither barren nor unfruitful in the knowledge of our Lord Jesus Christ."*
>
> ~ 2Peter 1:5-8 NKJV

United with the Body of Christ

> *"That they all may be one, as You, Father, are in Me, and I in You; that they also may be one in Us, that the world may believe that You sent Me."*
>
> ~ John 17:21 NKJV

Unity in Spirit

> *"With all lowliness and gentleness, with longsuffering, bearing with one another in love, endeavoring to keep the unity of the Spirit in the bond of peace. There is one body and one Spirit,*

just as you were called in one hope of your calling; one Lord, one faith, one baptism; one God and Father of all, who is above all, and through all, and in you all."

~ Ephesians 4:2-6 NKJV

United in Purpose

"And He Himself gave some to be apostles, some prophets, some evangelists, and some pastors and teachers, for the equipping of the saints for the work of ministry, for the edifying of the body of Christ, till we all come to the unity of the faith and of the knowledge of the Son of God, to a perfect man, to the measure of the stature of the fullness of Christ."

~ Ephesians 4:11-13 NKJV

Follow Christ's Example

"Him we preach, warning every man and teaching every man in all wisdom, that we may present every man perfect in Christ Jesus."

~ Colossians 1:28 NKJV

Know Doctrine

"But sanctify the Lord God in your hearts, and always be ready to give a defense to everyone who asks you a reason for the hope that is in you, with meekness and fear; having a good conscience, that when they defame you as evildoers, those who revile your good conduct in Christ may be ashamed."

~ 1Peter 3:15-16 NKJV

Ask yourself:

1. Identify and describe the maturity characteristics I possess.
2. Which fruit do I recognize can be improved in my life?

3. Describe how I can cultivate unity among my family, friends, church and workplace.

Pray

Father, I confess that change can be difficult but with You I can do anything. When I awaken each day, I ask You to make me keenly aware of my interactions with others. I want to be a faithful ambassador of the Lord. In Jesus' name. Amen.

Chapter 11
Response

"Now may the God of patience and comfort grant you to be like-minded toward one another, according to Christ Jesus."
~ Romans 15:5 NKJV

We have explored what the Bible teaches about offense and the symptoms. When believers take the position to remain in offense, they have allowed the Spirit of Offense to enter the mind and heart. This does not come from God. Once an unholy spirit affects you, you must take authority over it in order to walk in freedom. Before taking authority, you must confront what is happening. First, you have to acknowledge that an offense has occurred. Second, there must be a deliberate discovery of why the incident caused you to be offended. Then you can grasp the prospect of choosing what to do with the offense. There are three options to resolve this problem. Option one is to overlook the offense. This requires a conscious decision to refuse offense to be admitted to the heart and mind. The next option is to confront the offender. Finally, the third option is to refuse to overlook or confront the offense, choosing instead to hold onto it.

Option 1 – Overlook the Offense

"The discretion of a man makes him slow to anger, and his glory is to overlook a transgression."
~ Proverbs 19:11 NKJV

Each time a person feels offended, it does not call for confrontation. Believers are not called to be passive, neither are they called to be petty. There is a clear difference between the two. The writer of Proverbs makes an impressive declaration about the outcome of using wisdom and self-control when you have the opportunity to be offended. This perspective is a stark contrast to what is common. If you embrace the Proverbs teachings, you quickly see that God makes it clear that we are to make a choice in how we are to live. Our decisions will be known to be wise or foolish. If we are wise, we consider the knowledge we have of a matter, then arrive at our conclusions based on that knowledge.

If we are foolish, then we have knowledge and refuse to use it. There isn't a gray line down the middle. Let's reference *"a person's wisdom yields patience"* as a start. The virtue of patience usually has to be developed in someone's life. That person has learned the importance of being still and waiting for peace. You may ask the question, "Don't they want more facts and information?" Sometimes more information is helpful and other times it isn't. The craftiness of the enemy can create an illusion that appears to be right and it can be all wrong. When the fruit of patience has manifested in your life you are prone to allow time to run its course and you refrain from being hasty, which leads to regret.

The second part of the verse reads, *"It's to one's glory to overlook an offense."* In layman's terms, the phrase means, "It's to your advantage to overlook what happened." The church is hungry to learn how to effectively handle adversity. The world is known to operate in a climate of insults, revenge, betrayals, and schemes. The Body of Christ is to set a different standard. Foolish people are quick to anger, quick to jump to conclusions, quick to make poor choices, and love to fight. This does not come from the Holy Spirit; this is from the enemy. James says, *"Where do wars and fights come from among you? Do they not come from your desires for pleasure that war in your members?"* (Ja 4:1 NKJV). This is an issue of the heart and principle. A person who overlooks must have the heart to turn it over to the Lord and leave it there. Certainly, this is easier said than done, but it can be achieved.

Jesus is our example. He was without sin, a perfect man. He was confronted with offense on a continual basis, especially at the end of his earthly life. For us, we sin every day, often giving reason or provoking conflict in our lives. Long before Christ came Isaiah the prophet proclaimed: *"He was oppressed and He was afflicted, yet He opened not His mouth; and as a sheep before its shearers is silent, so He opened not His mouth"* (Is 53:7 NKJV). I can testify of the inward struggle to maintain my silence when offended.

God gently placed me in a situation to test and weed my heart. I was tested in my commitment to the Lord. The question became, "Will you honor me despite how you are being spoken to? Can you trust Me to keep and cover you?" I submitted to the Lord. As I was being tested, the Holy Spirit was pulling out the weeds in my heart through each insult. In a sense, I learned how to pray and love my enemies. The result is overwhelming because I became a firsthand witness of what it means to *"do unto others what you would have them do unto you"* (Matt 7:12). It is not about how we feel but more so about what the Lord requires.

By no means am I saying we are to always overlook offenses. What I am saying is that we should be able to "cast an offense on God" and be sincerely satisfied that He is enough to handle it. Peter encouraged, *"For this is commendable, if because of conscience toward God one endures grief, suffering wrongly. For what credit is it if, when you are beaten for your faults, you take it patiently? But when you do good and suffer if you take it patiently, this is commendable before God"* (1Pe 2:19-20 NKJV). When a person hasn't done anything to warrant attacks, criticisms, or rude behavior, God is taking record of the offender's behavior and the offended.

Many believers deal with undeserved mistreatment by others and have learned the value of meekness. The meek acknowledge their value and power, yet they make the conscious decision to be controlled by the Holy Spirit. If you walk in meekness, then you will find that God will raise your silent witness in the earth. People will take notice of God working in you. This one factor has the power to turn hopeless situations into great displays of God's goodness. Practicing meekness gives one the strength to refrain from reacting in tempting situations. More so, you will come to embrace the fact that this is not about you and the offender, but you and God.

Overlooking an offense is not an acceptance, but a rejection of the offense. The Lord esteems this as a valuable virtue. Anyone can misuse their power over another person, but everyone does not have the inner strength to overlook the abuser. Overlooking an offense requires the person to step outside of self and embrace the understanding that whatever has been said or done is not about him personally, but it is about bringing glory to the name of the Lord by being silent. We must be assured that there is a time to speak and a time to be silent. *"For to this you were called, because Christ also suffered for us, leaving us an example, that you should follow His steps"* (1Pe 2:21 NKJV).

Option 2 - Biblical Confrontation

"Brethren, if a man is overtaken in any trespass, you who are spiritual restore such a one in a spirit of gentleness, considering yourself lest you also be tempted."

~ Galatians 6:1 NKJV

When a person is unable to overlook an offense, a confrontation is necessary. For many, confrontation is an uncomfortable act of the will. The discomfort may be due to personality, the relational dynamics, or the result of feeling intimidated by the offender. In either case, believers are to follow God's advice to Joshua to be "strong and courageous" by dealing with the offender directly. 2 Timothy 1:7 says, *"For God has not given us a spirit of fear and timidity, but of power, love and self-discipline"* (NLT). We should never forfeit our peace over a matter. Confrontation must be handled by the leading of the Holy Spirit, otherwise it isn't fruitful.

Wisdom and discernment are to be employed and it begins with prayer. An adage says, "Prayer may not change the situation, but it will change you in the situation." When we bathe conflict in sincere prayer, we are allowing the Lord to intervene. The correct posture is to give the burden to the Lord and ask for Him to show you what is within your own heart first. At this point, you may be raising your defense wall and questioning why I am saying this. Prayer is a method of warfare. You must be able to recognize who or what the enemy is. Is the enemy a person? Is the enemy what was said or done? Is the enemy what you think about what was said or done? What is the enemy trying to do? How will the confrontation affect your future? Hence, we must allow the Lord to deal with our hearts first. Jeremiah the prophet says the heart is wicked and deceitful (Jer 17:9). Not going to God when emotions are high is a sure way to misunderstand or miss the Lord's leading.

When a person is committed to honoring his feelings, he is bound for failure. You can never trust how you feel because it is subject to change daily, based on inner and outside influences. I like to use the example of family relationships. Growing up with siblings there is always opportunity for some friction that will test your love for them. Although you may not feel the warm fuzzies deep within you, you know that you love them. That's why you are quick to drop the friction and go into war mode when the sibling is threatened. "Oh no you didn't! Not on my watch. That is MY brother!" The Lord is the same way about His children. He will stand up for us, despite how He feels about our behavior. *"But You, O Lord, are a God full of compassion, and gracious, longsuffering and abundant in mercy and truth"* (Ps 86:15 NKJV).

As believers, we are to be intentional in how we approach others in these types of adversarial situations. When Christians come to me struggling to forgive others, I share four commands to steer them toward the cross. Pray. Forgive. Bless. Love.

PRAY

"But I say unto you, love your enemies, bless them that curse you, do good to them that hate you, and **pray for them which despitefully use you, and persecute you.***"*

~ Matthew 5:44 NKJV

FORGIVE

"And whenever you stand praying, if you have anything against anyone, **forgive him***, that your Father in heaven may also forgive you your trespasses. But if you do not forgive, neither will your Father in heaven forgive your trespasses."*

~ Mark 11:25-26 NKJV

BLESS

Bless those *who persecute you; bless and do not curse.*

~ Romans 12:14 NKJV

LOVE

"But I say to you who hear, **love your enemies***, do good to those who hate you."*

~ Luke 6:27 NKJV

We – the Church – are without excuse. When you spend time reading these verses in context, you will recognize that God is serious about two relationships; our relationship with Him and our relationships with one another. The cross is the spiritual symbol to demonstrate the vertical and horizontal connections. We are unable to have right standing with God and unrighteous standing with His people. No matter the list of excuses we use, we are unable to change the truth of God's Word. Believers should be willing to accept the Lord's will for us. There must be a deep and abiding reverence for the Word of God. The perfect picture is when Jesus was in the Garden. In His humanity he clearly didn't want to go through the pending agony of the cross, but He said these words, *"Father, if it is Your will…"* (Lk 22:42 NKJV). Through embarrassment, anger and pain, we are to put our faith in God and aim to please Him. God will be faithful to empower you to release the offense if you will be faithful to believe Him.

Biblical Conflict Resolution

"Blessed are the peacemakers, for they shall be called sons of God."

~ Matthew 5:9 NKJV

Jesus understood men and their ways. He spent time addressing how kingdom citizens are to be distinguished from those outside, in darkness. The Lord provides a methodical outline for handling the conflicts we wage against one another. When offense happens, it does not have to mean that sin has been committed against another. We must keep in mind that every offense is not intended to do harm. It is quite possible to offend another person without having any knowledge of it. Thus, we know there is an inclination to sin if the offended is unable to overlook the offense, even if it was not intentional. No one is exempt from offending another person. This is an important factor to always keep in mind. Many people offer mercy to us that we are unconsciously aware of.

One sign of kingdom citizenship is to have the nature of a peacemaker. Unfortunately, many misunderstand the peacemaker's role. First, the peacemaker should have the inner peace which comes from the Lord, *"And the peace of God, which surpasses all understanding, will guard your hearts and minds through Christ Jesus"* (Phil 4:7 NKJV). This is the peace that enables you to love your friends and enemies, and it urges you to trust God over selfish motives. Second, the peacemaker ought to be led by the Spirit of God. If not, the actions or words of a peacemaker can cause an offense to escalate. Always consider that the peacemaker is to "make peace" in an adversarial situation. For this reason, it is important to caution "peacemakers" to test themselves before intervening.

It is God who knows the heart of every person, man does not. If we consult the Lord about what appears to be the obvious response to an offense, He may lead us to pray, watch and wait, then at the appointed time, He will lead us to speak. Before intervening, ask these questions of yourself: Has God told you to get involved? Are you unbiased? Do you hear with the Spirit? How well do you understand the motives of the opposing parties? Do you feel a "rush" to get involved? I would love to say that anytime you have the opportunity to intervene we should do so, but I won't. Certain situations are to be handled in the moment and some require the interception of God's wisdom and timing.

> *"Moreover, if your brother sins against you, go and tell him his fault, between you and him alone. If he hears you, you have gained your brother. But if he will not hear, take with you one or two more, that 'by the mouth of two or three witnesses every word may be established.' And if he refuses to hear them, tell it to the church. But if he refuses even to hear the church, let him be to you like a heathen and a tax collector."*
>
> ~ Matthew 18:15-17 NKJV

Biblical Steps to Resolve Conflict/Offense

Step 1 – Matthew 18:15a   Go to the offender in private

> *"Moreover, if your brother sins against you, go and tell him his fault, between you and him alone."*

This is a time to consider how you would like to be treated if you were the one who has been charged with offending another person. By meeting in private, both parties can address the issue face-to-face without interference from another party.

Advice: Refrain from discussing the matter with anyone other than the offender. This includes social media and other believers.

Step 2 – Matthew 18:15b-16   Take another brother with you

> *"If he hears you, you have gained your brother. But if he will not hear, take with you one or two more, that 'by the mouth of two or three witnesses every word may be established.'"*

You must be willing to accept that you may not be able to resolve or reason with the offender. Unfortunately, offense can expose misunderstandings or pride. Carrying another mature and Christ-minded individual with you to mediate the discussion is wise. This is not a time to bring people into the discussion who will merely side with you. This is a loving attempt to resolve a hurtful situation peacefully with the goal of forgiveness and reconciliation.

Advice: Prayerfully choose who will accompany you while confronting the offender. If the person is not a mature and unbiased saint, do not take them with you. Consider what Paul writes in Ephesians 4:25-5:4.

Step 3 – Matthew 18:17   Bring the offense to Church leadership

> *"And if he refuses to hear them, tell it to the church. But if he refuses even to hear the church, let him be to you like a heathen and a tax collector."*

Taking the issue to church leadership is for the purpose of changing the heart of the offender. This step should begin after a suitable time of intercession for the parties involved. Prayer should be targeted for repentance and forgiveness of the offender and offended.

Advice: This is not for the leaders or congregation to turn against the offender. By the time the confrontation has reached this step, both parties may need to be reminded of how the Lord regards sin between the brethren. (Refer to Galatians 6:1)

Option 3- Hold onto the Offense

"Looking carefully lest anyone fall short of the grace of God; lest any root of bitterness springing up cause trouble, and by this many become defiled."

~ Hebrews 12:15 NKJV

Dealing with offense is a natural part of our Christian walk. How we choose to handle offense makes the difference in our position before God and man. The person who chooses to hold the offense is in a compromised position and dire need of deliverance. As discussed earlier, an offense is an individual event that has occurred. We have the choice to overlook, confront, or hold the offense. When we hold the offense, it has become a companion in life. This is when the Spirit of Offense has worked its way to be a stronghold in the mind of the offended. It is contaminated thinking, or an incorrect thinking pattern based on a believed lie from the enemy.

"Always turn to God in the midst of your struggle and view people who offend you as an instrument of divine sovereignty."
~ John C. Maxwell

Paul explains to the Corinthians, *"Now whom you forgive anything, I also forgive. For if indeed I have forgiven anything, I have forgiven that one for your sakes in the presence of Christ, lest Satan should take advantage of us; for we are not ignorant of his devices"* (2Cor 2:10-11 NKJV). In context, Paul desires that as a community they are to forgive the one among them who has sinned, and he assures them that he shares in that forgiveness. Paul understood how the Body of Christ works. He knew that holding offense has the power to open the door to evil. He says, "for we are not ignorant of his designs." The enemy is a schemer.

Bitterness
Associated as symbolic of affliction, misery, and servitude.
~According to Easton's Bible Dictionary

When a believer is influenced or oppressed by the Spirit of Offense, a bitter root has been planted and nurtured in his heart. After Naomi's husband and sons died, she returned to Bethlehem as a very broken woman. As she was greeted by people she once knew, she identified herself according to her condition. *"Don't call me Naomi," she told them. "Call me Mara, for the Almighty has dealt very bitterly with me* "(Ru 1:20 NKJV). Ruth knew the Lord, but she had allowed the circumstances of life to determine her identity. She listened to the enemy's lies. She had become offended at God and the offense. Naomi's bitter state is a caution for us. We can surmise that Naomi's relationship with God and others changed. She had learned to live with disappointment and pain, believing the enemy's lies that things would not turn around for her again. She spoke from a bitter heart.

When an offense occurs, it is an opportune time to fellowship with the enemy. He uses the tactics of deception, temptation, and accusation to gain access into your life. When the offending seed is planted, he begins to fertilize it with negative thoughts about you and the offender. Without being aware, the enemy can deceive, tempt and accuse the offender and the offended. This is not difficult work because your life is unprotected daily. Satan knows he has influence and endurance. This works to his advantage because he can record and rewind the reels of your life. He has watched you long enough to know your triggers; always looking for your sin of choice, weaknesses, and strengths.

Although he isn't privileged to your thoughts, he has an evil army assigned to follow you as you go about the affairs of life. Your target areas are the platforms for conversations with your imagination.

The way to prevent these dark discourses is to *"cast down arguments and every high thing that exalts itself against the knowledge of God, bringing every thought into captivity to the obedience of Christ"* (2Cor 10:5 NKJV). When you do not take authority over negative thoughts and emotions, the enemy has an open field. After long hours and days of meditating on his lies, Satan has gained territory. He is now working in and through you to separate you in your relationship with the offender and others. At this point, Satan's Spirit of Offense wants to use the offended to create more division.

> *"Be angry, and do not sin; do not let the sun go down on your wrath, nor give place to the devil."*
>
> ~ Ephesians 4:26 NKJV

The Spirit of Offense will convince you to separate yourself from anyone who tries to bring correction or truth to your situation. Ultimately, the offense that started out as a single event has grown into a way of life. The Spirit of Offense can lord over every relationship in your life, beyond that of the original offender. As division within the Body of Christ becomes more widespread, the church becomes more ineffective. When you hold the offense, you are giving the devil a foothold. Any response to offense costs you something because you have to give up one thing in order to gain something else.

Ask yourself:

1. When is the last time I was offended? What happened?
2. Describe how I would handle the situation differently today.
3. Explain how I can determine whether an offense is a petty issue or not.

Pray

Father, I recognize that each day I have the power to choose how I will respond to life's challenges. Today, I choose to reject the temptation to be petty. I refuse to magnify small and insignificant matters in my life. Thank You for blessing me with wisdom. In Jesus' name. Amen.

Chapter 12
Wounded Soul

"He restores my soul; He leads me in the paths of righteousness for His name's sake."

~ Psalm 23:3 NKJV

One reason people find it difficult to forgive an offender is they have experienced a wound to their soul. Soul wounds occur because of sin. Either someone sinned against you, or you sinned against someone else. This type of injury has a deep effect on the emotions of an individual and it makes it very difficult to release or let go of hurts. Unlike a physical wound, the soul is hidden from open view. For example, if you fall on broken glass and cut your arm you can see the wound heal. On the contrary, the soul wound is cloaked within the physical body, easily staying open without healing. This is especially hard for the one who has experienced trauma. The unpleasant memory of the event serves as a reminder to hold onto the memory rather than severing the cord.

When we are offended, there is a natural inclination to react mentally or emotionally. These behaviors can be overt or subtle expressions of hurt. Most are rooted in childhood. Growing up, many children learned how to cope with their bruised emotions. These coping mechanisms range from ignoring, withdrawal, lashing out in anger, bullying, fighting, or crying. Left alone, any of these childish tactics will result in more dysfunction. We rarely find that immature methods of handling broken and damaged emotions work well. The Bible teaches that it's a man's discretion that makes him slow to anger. In the Hebrew, the meaning of discretion points to one who exercises prudence or insight. The discreet person operates with an effective measure of wisdom and self-control, which restrains him from impulsive or irrational anger. The principle is that we are to employ reason in our response to issues that provoke negativity. Unfortunately, we often justify our hurt feelings and emotions based on what happened and how we feel about it, without consulting the long-range impact of the behavior. A wounded soul is an open door for the enemy to disturb our peace and hold us hostage to past hurts.

> *"Now may the God of peace Himself sanctify you completely; and may your whole spirit, soul, and body be preserved blameless at the coming of our Lord Jesus Christ."*
> ~ 1Thessalonians 5:23 NKJV

Paul recognizes man as being triune or having three components. He prays that God will sanctify man's spirit, soul and body. By this time in Paul's life, he has confronted the inner casualties of war. He is consciously aware of the evil he inflicted upon others, prior to Christ and how the Lord had to remove, or set him apart, to change him. Now, in retrospect, he offers his witness of God's power to do a complete work in his life. He looks to the Lord as the Source of bringing healing and wholeness to the total person. The person who is being sanctified can be compared to a house. The physical body, man's house, is visible to the naked eye. Within the body are the senses, systems and organs. The body is how we function in the world around us. The unseen components are the spirit and soul, like the air.

The spirit of man is the deepest level of our existence because here is where we find meaning and purpose in life. One of Job's friends related it as, *"But it is the spirit in a person, the breath of the Almighty, that gives them understanding"* (Job 32:8 NIV). The Hebrew word for the spirit is *ruach* (rü'·akh), meaning breath or wind. Before man was formed, the *"ruach"* of God *"was hovering over the face of the waters"* (Gen 1:2). This is significant in that it is the first reference in the Bible to the Holy Spirit. He, the Spirit, was readying Himself to create life on earth. Imagine an eagle watching over his young birds, as they are prepared to leave the nest, he catches them if they fall (Deut 32:11-12). The same Holy Spirit continues to move, or hover, over mankind today. This divine Force is the very source of life. Without this *"ruach"* there is death.

During the creation process, God breathed into man and he became a living soul (Gen 2:7). What was breathed into man? Life. The Old Testament word meaning soul is *"ne'phesh"* (neh'.fesh).[26] God literally imparted His divine image and likeness into man. What originated as a cold sculpture of clay became a warm, lively, breathing being. God's breath provided the bridge for man to connect with his Creator. This relationship generates the conscious, will and reasoning of man. Until the dreadful garden drama, the "ruach" of God in mankind was in congruence with God. Sin interrupted this harmony. By God's grace at salvation, the spirit of man is born again and redeemed. We can communicate with God by the spirit; therefore, I refer to the spirit of man as the unseen bridge that connects us to God. When we are born again, Satan is unable to touch our spirit, so he works through the soul.

The invisible soul houses the mind, will, and emotions of man. This word suggests possessing life. In a similar meaning, the New Testament word for soul is *"psyche,"* which references the whole person. Man's physical body connects to the world through the senses, which are experienced within the soul. This connection handles how we interpret what we feel. Within the soul is where we find ourselves trusting or not trusting God. Here is where we choose whether to worship Him. It is not wise to live our lives by the dictates of our soul because it leads to being more inwardly focused, leaving less room for contact with God.

It is important that we understand that our soul is central, but it is not the core of who we are. The deepest place of our being is the spiritual heart. After Nathan confronted David about his sin, he asked the Lord to remake his heart. In his brokenness, he acknowledged, *"Behold, You desire truth in the innermost being"* (Ps 51:6

---

[26] https://www.blueletterbible.org/lang/lexicon/lexicon.cfm?t=kjv&strongs=h5315

NKJV). Our spiritual heart and soul are so interconnected that it is often difficult to discern whether the soul or spirit is leading us. The spiritual heart is the source wherein all issues of life flow, so it must be protected (Prov 4:23). Concerning the heart, the Lord told Ezekiel, *"I will give them an undivided heart and put a new spirit in them; I will remove from them their heart of stone and give them a heart of flesh"* (Ez 11:19 NIV). It is God's Word that separates spirit from soul, allowing us to be led by the spirit. (See Appendix C)

> *"All great Christians have been wounded souls."*
> ~ A. W. Tozer

Soul wounds literally become a part of us when they have existed for a long time. When we are born again, it does not mean that our emotional – soul wounds – are instantly healed. Most often, the superficial scratches can be healed in time, but the larger abrasions in the soul usually require attention beyond self. We must not deny what has happened to us and that we need to be restored. A key sign of living with a wounded soul is when a believer does not reach a place of walking in victory in Christ. This does not suggest anyone will have a trouble-free life. It means that the person with a wounded soul will relate a large part of their perceptual beliefs to what he has experienced in the past. He will read the Word of God about certain things and acknowledge that it's true. Then he will deny that it is true in his situation. Many times, he will respond to God's Word with "But, the last time…" These wounds have a way of changing who we are and how we see life. Many bow to the wound by accepting it to be how they have been wired. This is not so. We must remember that a wounded soul is rooted in sin.

> *"For the word of God is living and powerful, and sharper than any two-edged sword, piercing even to the division of soul and spirit, and of joints and marrow, and is a discerner of the thoughts and intents of the heart."*
> ~ Hebrews 4:12 NKJV

God's Word has the power to heal and set us free. We can embrace the Word or reject it, but there are great benefits to receiving the truth. The Hebrew writer describes God's Word as being *"sharper than any double-edged sword."* When the Word is read or heard, it literally separates what is in the soul from what is of the spirit. Take a moment and picture a sharp sword piercing your body when you read God's Word concerning your issues. As the blade penetrates your flesh, you experience the pain caused by the incision. While the sword travels to the wounds of your soul, discomfort increases because memories are revisited. The anointed sword – Word of God – begins to release a healing balm that flows to the inner scrapes, breaks, blows and bruises. As the sword exits the body it acts as a laser light, healing both the physical body and the soul. We don't always like the way we feel when the Word of God brings correction and conviction, but when we obey the Scripture healing takes place.

> *"Beloved, I pray that you may prosper in all things and be in health, just as your soul prospers."*
>
> ~ 3John 2 NKJV

If you have a history of harboring negative emotions in your heart, your soul needs to be healed, or delivered. The symptoms of a wounded soul are very similar to those walking in the Spirit of Offense. The main distinction between the two is that the symptoms of the Spirit of Offense are directed towards the offender. With the wounded soul, the wound is the focus. This is why it is so dangerous. The adage "hurt people, hurt people" is true. The wound that remains unhealed, exposes the soul to the schemes of the enemy. Once he has entered, the wound has become an altar within your soul. This demonic trapping corrupts your heart, alters your thinking and blinds your vision, often leading people to abuse, commit crimes, or harm self. Instead of being led by the Holy Spirit, the wound controls your life.

Jacob's House

"But when his brothers saw that their father loved him more than all his brothers, they hated him and could not speak peaceably to him."

~ Genesis 37:4 NKJV

As I study the Scriptures, I like to place myself in the landscape of the text. For example, when I read the Gospels, I sometimes imagine myself as a person in the crowd, watching every detail of how Jesus handles the disciples and those who are sick among him. When reading about the Exodus, I have been one of the mothers instructing her children to quiet down and listen as they gathered their belongings to leave Egypt. Unlike the other texts, reading about Joseph seems to speak to the gift of discernment within me. Most sermons focus on Joseph as the favorite son, being sold into slavery, and how God reversed the brothers' evil for Joseph's good. I see something else. Although he held his composure, as he encountered the brothers who mistreated him, he also faced the wounds of his past.

Joseph was 17 years old when his brothers sold him into slavery. From that day, his life was profoundly altered. In despair, he was torn away from the security of his family, despite their jealousy toward him. He knew he had the love of his father and other family members. Through it all, God was with him and His favor caused Joseph to overcome every obstacle he faced. Years later, Joseph had two sons. The first is Manasseh, meaning *"For God has made me forget all my toil and all my father's house"* (Gen 41:51 NKJV). The younger is Ephraim, *"For God has caused me to be fruitful in the land of my affliction"* (Gen 41:52 NKJV). These names are symbolic of the pain and suffering he had endured. With each passing day, I believe Joseph wondered why he was so hated by his brothers. Perhaps he thought about why he told them about his dreams. Maybe he never understood why the dreams generated so much resentment. Did he know why he was treated better than his brothers? I believe the answers to these questions were revealed over the years although the wounds were not healed.

Commentators have questioned Joseph's actions because there isn't any scriptural evidence supporting effort on Joseph's part to contact his family. Joseph was no different than we are today. When a person is wounded without any means to resolve the offense, an inward dialogue continues between the offense and the wound. As the story reads, when Joseph's brothers showed up in Egypt to buy food, he recognized them, but he didn't disclose his identity to them. He helped them, but in an effort to see his brother Benjamin, he would not allow Reuben to leave. When the brothers returned with Benjamin, Joseph invited them to his home for dinner and he planted a silver cup in his sack. Upon their discovery of the "hidden cup" Joseph retained Benjamin as his slave.

Through all the conversations, Joseph continued to conceal his identity. Then, he overheard his brothers describing the day they watched their younger brother cry when they sold him away. They still didn't know the Prime Minister was the brother they sold. Neither did they realize that he could understand their conversation. The Bible says that when Joseph overheard, he *"turned himself away and wept"* (Gen 42:24). It is noted that he cried again when he finally saw his brother named Benjamin. Eventually, the tension elevated between Joseph and his brothers and he was unable to control his emotions any longer (Gen 45).

The narrative is a dramatic portrayal of family offense. Despite the years of separation between Jacob, his sons and Joseph, they all lived with wounded souls. Jacob was guilty of planting the seed of rejection in their hearts. Instead of embracing all his sons, he showed favoritism to Joseph and Benjamin, especially Joseph. Jacob's partiality resulted in a household of anger, bitterness, resentfulness and jealousy amongst siblings. Until they were confronted with Joseph as their brother, they resigned to living the lie they had told their dad 21 years prior. When the brothers got to Egypt, Joseph recognized them, but they didn't recognize him. He used their inability to distinguish him to his advantage in order to test their motives.

> *"The soul feels what the mind ignores."* ~ Unknown

As surely as Joseph was testing them, he was being tested himself. It appears that Joseph was torn between giving in to his emotions of anger, hurt and revenge and honoring God. Outwardly, Joseph was unrecognizable; he no longer looked like the Jewish teenager they sold away. He was a grown man who had weathered the issues of life. Joseph had learned how to handle himself in a foreign land and earn the respect of leaders. He walked in favor and gained political status. Inwardly, Joseph struggled with the unresolved emotional pain of his past. It's possible that he carried the mental picture of the day his brothers watched him being taken away. The memory of being his father's favorite son may have produced an incredible guilt in his consciousness that told him he deserved what happened to him. Though he was strong, he was wounded and so were his brothers.

Signs and Symptoms of Soul Wounds

> *"He heals the brokenhearted and binds up their wounds."*
> ~ Psalm 142:7 NKJV

Angry with God
Blames God for what has happened in his life.

Self-Anger/Self Hate
Believe that he deserves what has happened to him. This is very common in people who experience sexual violation as children.

Hard to forgive
Seems almost impossible to forgive others.

Little Patience
The person has little tolerance with other people's shortcomings.

Sensitive Emotions
This person displays quick feelings of anger, bitterness, jealousy and rage at small incidents.

Stay in the Past
The mention of a past event triggers deep emotions of hurt, sadness or anger.

Achievement and Perfectionist Driven
To fill a void the person develops an obsession with accomplishment in the form of education, career, social status, positions, and titles.

Commitment and Love Issues
Hard to accept genuine love from others.

Lack of Peace
Becomes agitated and frustrated easily.

Vengeful
The built-up anger and resentment make him retaliate easily.

Reckless lifestyle
Found in feeding the flesh with food, smoking, drugs, porn, drinking or any vice that can potentially become an addiction.

Unreasonable Expectations of Others
Set very high standards for others and get quickly disappointed when they are not met.

This list is not exhaustive.

Ask yourself:

1. What wound have I protected by ignoring or acting tough?
2. What area of my life do I refer to when justifying why I won't forgive someone? Why?
3. Describe how God's Word is "setting me free" from the wounds of my past.

Pray

Father, I desire to my heart to be healed everywhere it hurts. I give you every toxic emotion and memory that has lingered in my soul. Fill me with Your healing balm that heals and covers every wound. As I am healed, I shall bring healing to others. In Jesus' name. Amen.

Chapter 13
Working Together

"And we know that all things work together for good to those who love God, to those who are the called according to His purpose."

~ Romans 8:28 NKJV

I have come to realize that nothing in life goes unnoticed or wasted by the Lord. Whether someone deliberately sins against you or you neglect to do as you should, it all serves a purpose in your life. I am reminded of Job's experience and how the Lord had a conversation with the enemy. Satan knew Job was a child of God and recognized His protection over his life. What he did not understand is the depth of Job's loving commitment to God. Ironically, it was God who suggested Job for the testing: *"Then the LORD said to Satan, 'Have you considered My servant Job, that there is none like him on the earth, a blameless and upright man, one who fears God and shuns evil? And still he holds fast to his integrity, although you incited Me against him, to destroy him without cause.'"* (Job 2:3 NKJV). Think about this, perhaps you are struggling with an offense because God whispered your name to the enemy.

For many years, I wondered why the Lord would do such a thing to one of his best servants. It seems unfair, unjust, and unreasonable for one person to have endured so much. If there wasn't a good reason for an attack, then why did it have to go so far? Perhaps you are praying for your marriage to no avail because on the surface it looks like you have reached an impasse. You ask, "Can it get any worse?" Sometimes it does. Why did that new husband have to lose his wife to cancer? Why did my friend lose his job within 30 days of buying his new home? Why? Certainly, each of us has experienced something we believe is wrong and yet it did not destroy our faith. It is because God uses the darkest and most painful situations to change us from within. If we had the exclusive rights to self-transformation, we would always choose the painless, simple and shortest route. This road would leave us with a deficit of strength to build our faith. Many of us can testify that tears of anguish have served as the substance of transformation. Job was the model for us to follow.

Although he knew the goodness of the Lord, through his process, Job became weary. He lamented, *"My soul loathes my life; I will give free course to my complaint, I will speak in the bitterness of my soul"* (Job 10:1 NKJV). Ironically, we are the same way under much less intensity of loss. There is always the prevailing question of why. As we read the pages of Job's daunting situation, we are introduced to ourselves. There are times when something will happen, and it leaves us struggling to find the meaning. It's in those moments that we are to remember David's words. *"It is good for me that I have been afflicted, that I may learn Your statutes"* (Ps 119:71 NKJV). David was overlooked by his father; hated by his father in law; he committed adultery and murder; he lived as a fugitive due to jealousy; was assigned to minister to a madman; and he juggled leading a nation while claiming husband to at least eight wives, yet he continued to pursue God. However, David dealt with the pains of affliction at the hands of others and himself. Many of his difficulties could be traced back to his choices. Like David, we absorb a clearer image of the great I Am when we look for Him in our distress.

The Apostle Paul was emphatic in his statement, *"And we know that in all things God works for the good of those who love him, who have been called according to his purpose"* (Ro 8:28 NKJV). What is good about someone cheating on you? Your house being destroyed in a hurricane? What is good about going through a bitter divorce? A baby dying? A sudden paralysis? There are unlimited circumstances which have the ability to call our faith into question. Sometimes the complexity of an offense does the same thing. Perhaps the offense came from a spouse or parent, or someone you dared to believe could never mistreat you. Even under the worst circumstances, Paul is saying it is working – the offense – for your good. The conditions are simple. Love God. Be called according to His purpose. Loving God seems easy, but is it? For starters, we do not love God how we want to, we are to love Him by His standards. Many times, I have repeated the adage, "Action speaks louder than words. Love is not what you say but all about what you do." God says, *"If you love Me, keep my commandments"* (John 14:15 NKJV). When you love the Lord, the proof is found in honoring His Word. This love also serves as a link to His will for your life. Sincere love for the Lord creates a desire to please Him. We please Him in releasing anything that would hinder us from receiving His grace.

 The outcome of Job's situation is powerful and beautiful. The power of the narrative is found in the hidden treasures of darkness. His unwavering faith in God, despite his inability to find cause for his suffering is something to take notice of. As Job navigated through years of heartbreak, sickness, and judgmental comments from ignorant friends, he kept his faith in God when it seemed he could have lost all hope. He was resolute in his proclamation, *"But He knows the way that I take; when He has tested me, I shall come forth as gold"* (Job 23:10 NKJV). Job knew that God was with him in his deepest and darkest times, although he could not see the end, he knew it would prove to be priceless. He had to rely on God, trusting that what he was going through was far greater than his personal wellbeing and contentment. He compared his journey to the refining of gold, which takes place under the heat of fire. As the heat intensifies, dross rises to the top and is removed. Whatever lies within that shouldn't be with us, the fire of God removes it. He uses the heat of suffering, pain, broken relationships, neglect, abuse and offense, to expose and release it from our lives.

 The beauty of Job's ordeal is woven in the tapestry of God's total restoration. When the Lord restores, He does a complete work, affecting the entire person. The writer reports, *"And the Lord restored*

Job's losses when he prayed for his friends. Indeed, the Lord gave Job twice as much as he had before" (Job 42:10 NKJV). If we refuse to doubt Him, God strengthens our relationship with Him, increases our usefulness, and gives us more than we lost. Whether Job ever received the answer he was looking for we don't know, but he passed the test with honors. Everything he faced worked out for his good and God's glory in the end.

The love of God sometimes ushers you to unknown places, through uncharted terrain. The rougher the course, the more you wonder whether you clearly heard the Lord's direction. I can remember a time I knew I was following the direction of the Holy Spirit and as I walked, it appeared that I was stepping in land mines all around me. Late one Sunday night I fell on my knees in angst, and I asked the Lord to let me know if I had missed Him. He quickly reminded me that, "*Jesus was led up by the Spirit into the wilderness to be tempted by the devi*l" (Matt 4:1 NKJV). Being led by the Spirit is not an exemption from trouble. The presence of trouble is often a signal of being on the right track. I discovered that I was able to recognize things that I would have overlooked if the landmines were not there. The delays proved to be opportunities to go deeper in prayer, to remove my robe of pride, and develop more dependency on the Lord. He began to connect and direct my steps, to get me through, to the place He had ordained for me. All the while, every bump, U-turn, mountain and rest stop, were working together for my good.

The phrase "for my good" has been a soothing balm for some weary days in my life. Paul wants us to grab hold of the overarching fact that the goodness of the Lord will not abandon us when we need Him the most. We must hold onto what we know about Him. He loves us unconditionally. He already knows what we will do before we do it. He is with us. We can trust Him. And finally, He is sovereign. The Lord knows what to do and allow for His will to be carried out. He is a masterful strategist. Think about it this way: If He never allows or orders the dirty, tough and ugly some would never read the Word and pray from the depths of the soul. It is a scientific fact that friction is a catalyst for change. As the people of

God, we are to embrace the power of His anointing that works within each of us. Three contrasting dynamics are at work at the same time. He is adding, subtracting and molding. As we spin on the Potter's wheel, keep in mind that while God is shaping us on the outside, He is also removing anything that does not belong within. He is creating vessels that won't bend, break or leak under the pressures of life. When we are offended, there is a reason we have responded negatively. This is the time to remember a crucial truth: "All things do work for our good if we truly love the Lord."

"It's like riding a rollercoaster from the backseat.
Even though you can't see what's ahead, you buckle up, close your eyes,
lift your arms and enjoy the thrill of the ride."
~ Margo W. Williams

If you stop and think about the value of your Christian experience, you will find that it is priceless. As you work through an offense, you gain access to a much deeper experience of God's love, forgiveness and sovereignty. Interestingly, in Romans, Paul confronted the Romans about their holier-than-thou attitudes about the Gentiles and their sin. He informed the Romans that everyone, including them, deserved God's judgment. In other words, they thought they were somehow worthy of escaping judgment for committing the same sin as others did. So, he asked the rhetorical question, *"Or do you despise the riches of His goodness, forbearance, and longsuffering, not knowing that the goodness of God leads you to repentance?"* (Ro 2:4 NKJV). The Romans were hypocritical. Paul wanted them to know that no one got a "free pass." He meant for them to be grateful for the Lord's mercy, which is given to all. Truly, when offended, it exposes the inner heart. We must allow our hearts to be cleansed by the Word of God so that we can appreciate what He has done for us, despite ourselves.

There is treasure in the unseen and dark places of life. Beauty that cannot be seen with the natural eye is viewed in the spirit. What we often believe is lacking is the one thing that tends to reveal value and purpose. I grew up watching the women in our family cook, my favorite was baking. My maternal grandmother would use a spoon and mix up a sweet bread that my grandfather called "sponge bread." The ingredients were simple: flour, old bread scraps, butter, sugar, eggs, milk and flavoring. During one visit, my granddaddy challenged me to make the "sponge bread" for him, so Grandma agreed to tell me what to do, but she wouldn't mix it for me.

I remember feeling focused and determined to make the "sponge bread" to my granddaddy's liking. When it came out of the oven I was thrilled because it looked and smelled delicious. I was so proud because I loved to receive his compliments. I spooned some of it on a saucer and added vanilla ice cream, the way he liked it served. He ate it and told me that I cooked just like my grandmother. I quickly fixed myself some, took a bite and at once knew I had left out a vital ingredient: the vanilla flavoring. I looked at granddaddy and asked, "Why did you tell me my bread tasted like Grandma's? You know it doesn't." He smiled and replied, "Once you eat that cream with it, it all works together fine." To my granddaddy, the vanilla flavoring did not make the "sponge bread" good, it was the love he had for the cook, so it all worked together.

The love we have for God and His Word creates the kind of faith that believes despite what is seen. One of my favorite songs is a testimony of Romans 8:28. The chorus says, *"All things are working for me, even things I can't see. Your ways are so beyond me, but You said that You would let it be for my good. So, I'll rest and just believe."*[27] Each time I listen to the lyrics I feel my soul leaping and weeping. I leap for joy that everything that has come against me has eventually fallen and been rendered powerless. The joy floods my soul as I am reminded that when God is for us, He is so much more than any enemy or demon (Ro 8:31). He uses it all to bring us to a place in Him that we have yet to discover, yet we are to believe.

---

[27] Hammond, Fred Hammond. "All Things Are Working." *Pages of Life: Chapters I & II,* Zomba Recording, 1998.

"What God has predestined for you is too big to be petty. Set your heart to believe beyond the offense because it's working for your good."
~ Margo W. Williams

It is with the heart that we accept that nothing is wasted because everything is working for our good. For the believer, God aims to get us to the place where we can be the most valuable, or useful, to Him. He wants to remove everything that we hold onto that would cause us to miss His best for our lives. The experience of walking out an offense is a divine strategy to expose the hidden issues of our hearts. God already knows it's there and He wants us to get rid of it.

Conform
Indicating an inner change of nature,
working into the outward life.[28]

When we struggle through the dark places, or wrestle to release ourselves from the grip of offense, the Lord's goal is change. Inward change. The belief that many believers confess is that God wants them to be happy. If you ascribe to this teaching, understand that this is poor biblical doctrine. God's concern has little to do with happiness and more to do with holiness. His primary concern is the believer's character. Therefore, the measures used to change us do not appeal to our soul, but strengthen the spirit. The dark times are God's factory of transformation. *"For whom He foreknew, He also predestined to become conformed to the image of His Son, that He might be the firstborn among many brethren"* (Ro 8:29 NKJV). Has your mind changed? Your habits? Your heart? Your priorities? Your witness?

The outcome has already been determined; we are predestined. The challenges, pain, and darkness we face are used to conform our character. We do not look like Jesus when we live with the symptoms that were discussed in chapter five. Paul is encouraging us to have a

---
[28] https://www.biblestudytools.com/encyclopedias/isbe/conform-conformable.html

higher view of God and our covenant rights in Him. Instead of believing the process is the end, we accept that it is part of the sacred journey to becoming more like Christ. When we successfully process through, we look more like Jesus.

If you are still having a tough time moving beyond offense, I ask you to consider three facts about God and your situation:

Fact 1: Nothing is Hidden from God

"For nothing is secret that will not be revealed, nor anything hidden that will not be known and come to light."

~ Luke 8:17 NKJV

"And there is no creature hidden from His sight, but all things are naked and open to the eyes of Him to whom we must give account."

~ Hebrews 4:13 NKJV

Fact 2: Suffering Comes with the Calling

"For to this you were called, because Christ also suffered for us, leaving us an example, that you should follow His steps."

~ 1Peter 2:21 NKJV

"In this you greatly rejoice, though now for a little while, if need be, you have been grieved by various trials, that the genuineness of your faith, being much more precious than gold that perishes, though it is tested by fire, may be found to praise, honor, and glory at the revelation of Jesus Christ."

~ 1Peter 1:6-7 NKJV

Fact 3: Trust God to Deal with the Offender

> *"Who, when He was reviled, did not revile in return; when He suffered, He did not threaten, but committed Himself to Him who judges righteously."*
>
> ~ 1Peter 2:23 NKJV

> *"For it is better, if it is the will of God, to suffer for doing good than for doing evil."*
>
> ~ 1Peter 3:17 NKJV

Ask yourself:

1. Describe a time I felt I did not deserve what happened to me.
2. Looking back on the situation, what is the lesson or blessing the Lord was teaching me about His character?
3. Describe what I have learned about myself during times of testing and trials.

Pray

Father, I recognize I have often overlooked the very things I should pay attention to. I want to take responsibility for how I feel and not place blame on others. Search me, Oh God, and show me what is hidden that I have overlooked in my life. I do not want to stumble. I commit myself to You and your will. In Jesus' name. Amen.

Chapter 14
Biblical Examples

"All Scripture is given by inspiration of God, and is profitable for doctrine, for reproof, for correction, for instruction in righteousness."

~ 2Timothy 3:16 NKJV

Jesus made it clear that offense is a normal part of community (Lk 17:1). As you read the Bible, you will discover various adversarial relationships due to some type of sin, betrayal, misunderstanding or confrontation. Each circumstance hails a different outcome. Scripture teaches us, *"For whatever things were written before were written for our learning, that we through the patience and comfort of the Scriptures might have hope"* (Ro 15:4 NKJV). Some of God's most useful servants conquered offenses. With each profile listed below, their experiences were instrumental in perfecting their character for increased usefulness in the Kingdom. Below are a few of my favorite narratives, which shed light on the community of faith and the pettiness of offense. Imagine yourself as being a character in the text. Ask yourself how you would handle this situation better.

Cain and Abel

"Abel also brought of the firstborn of his flock and of their fat. And the Lord respected Abel and his offering, but He did not respect Cain and his offering. And Cain was very angry, and his countenance fell."

~ Genesis 4:4-5 NKJV

The Offense

This is an amazing account of the first two brothers recorded in Scripture. Cain, a farmer, and Abel, a shepherd. Cain became offended at God and his brother. Abel offered the Lord a sacrifice of his best: his firstborn sheep. Cain, who had the same opportunity, chose otherwise. When God accepted Abel's offering, Cain became jealous and angry. He was deeply offended.

The Motive

Rather than dealing with the outcome of his own decision, he chose to kill his brother.

Outcome

When God questioned him about the whereabouts of Abel, he was evasive in responding. It was not until he learned of his punishment that he appeared to have any remorse.

Sarai and Hagar

"So, he went in to Hagar, and she conceived. And when she saw that she had conceived, her mistress became despised in her eyes."

~ Genesis 16:4 NKJV

The Offense

Sarai was unable to conceive, and she offered her servant to her husband. He accepted the offer and the servant conceived. Afterwards, Sarai felt guilt and jealousy toward Hagar, her servant.

The Motive

God had promised to bless Abram and Sarai with a child (Gen 15:4). As Sarai waited to become pregnant, she became disillusioned. She didn't want the stigma associated with being barren and she had stopped trusting the Lord.

Outcome

God supported both mothers and made nations of both sons. To Hagar the Angel of the Lord said, "*I will give you more descendants than you can count*" (Gen 16:10 NLT). Hagar's son, Ishmael, became the father of the Arab nations and Islamic world. Sarah's son, Isaac, became noted as a patriarch of the nation of Israel. To this day there has never been a peaceful resolve between the descendants of Isaac and Ishmael.

Joseph and Mary

> *"Now the birth of Jesus Christ was as follows: After His mother Mary was betrothed to Joseph, before they came together, she was found with child of the Holy Spirit. Then Joseph, her husband, being a just man, and not wanting to make her a public example, was minded to put her away secretly."*
>
> ~ Matthew 1:18-19 NKJV

The Offense

Joseph and Mary were engaged to marry and never had intercourse. Ironically, she conceived a child.

Motive

Joseph knew that if Mary was with child, he could not have been the father. According to the Mosaic Law, if it was revealed that

Mary had committed adultery, she could have been stoned to death. He was also challenged by the claim that the Holy Spirit impregnated Mary. Joseph knew he had to make a choice to avoid the stigma of Mary's seeming unfaithfulness to him.

Outcome

Joseph was noted to be just in his dealings, and he displayed great love for Mary. The Bible says that he didn't want to make a public example of Mary (Matt 1:19). God's messenger counseled, *"Joseph, son of David, do not be afraid to take Mary as your wife, for that which is conceived in her is of the Holy Spirit"* (Matt 1:20). Joseph stayed with Mary and became the earthly father to Jesus.

Paul and John Mark

> *"Now Barnabas was determined to take with them John called Mark. But Paul insisted that they should not take with them the one who had departed from them in Pamphylia, and had not gone with them to the work. Then the contention became so sharp that they parted from one another. And so, Barnabas took Mark and sailed to Cyprus."*
> ~ Acts 15:37-39 NKJV

Offense

John Mark went with Paul and Barnabas on the first missionary journey. When they reached their second stop, John Mark deserted them and returned to Jerusalem. Paul was greatly disturbed by John Mark's actions.

Motive

Paul and Barnabas were both committed to doing the Lord's work. They disagreed on whether John Mark should be given another opportunity to serve on the team. Paul refused to allow him to serve with them again.

Outcome

God is glorified when there is unity in the midst of division. Both men honored their personal convictions to the Lord and God blessed their obedience. No doubt John Mark learned the seriousness of ministry from Paul and Barnabas. This separation was a divine cooperative effort for the advancement of the Kingdom. At the end of Paul's life, he asked that John Mark come visit him, *"Get Mark and bring him with you, for he is useful to me for ministry"* (2 Tim 4:11b NKJV). I believe Paul eventually understood that God was also using John Mark to spread the gospel. Paul released the offense.

Pharisees and Sadducees

> *"Then His disciples came and said to Him, 'Do You know that the Pharisees were offended when they heard this saying?'"*
> ~ Matthew 15:12 NKJV

Offense

Jesus' words dealt with the heart. These men were filled with pride, greed and power. They resisted the teaching because it exposed their dark hearts and challenged their authority among the people.

Motive

Jesus was teaching and preaching the good news of the Kingdom, correcting false doctrine.

Outcome

Jesus was crucified. Through his death and resurrection, we have eternal life. The resurrection of Jesus proved to destroy the criticism and lies of the Pharisees. *"I tell you the truth, unless a kernel of wheat is planted in soil and dies, it remains alone. But its death will produce many new kernels – a plentiful harvest of new lives"* (John 12:24NLT).

Mary and Martha

"But Martha was distracted with much serving, and she approached Him and said, 'Lord, do You not care that my sister has left me to serve alone? Therefore, tell her to help me.'"

Luke 10:40 NKJV

Offense

While Martha was preparing a meal to serve Jesus and the disciples, her sister Mary stayed in the room and listened to Jesus teach. This frustrated Martha and she asked Jesus to intervene. Her tone was disrespectful toward Jesus.

Motive

Both sisters had good intentions with what they were doing. Martha was being hospitable, but she believed Mary's priorities were out of order.

Outcome

Jesus responded to Martha without getting emotional. He didn't address her attitude, instead He spoke about their actions. He corrected Martha by saying, *"Martha, Martha, you are worried and troubled about many things. But one thing is needed, and Mary has chosen that good part, which will not be taken away from her"* (Lk 10:41-42). Jesus' rebuke revealed the hidden issue of Martha's heart: misplaced priorities.

Judas and the Woman with the Alabaster Box

"Why was this fragrant oil not sold for three hundred denarii and given to the poor?"

~ John 12:5 NKJV

Offense

When Mary took the expensive oil and began to anoint the feet of Jesus, Judas was offended because he felt it could have been sold for money.

Motive

Mary's heart was full of gratitude and love for what Jesus had done for her. Judas wanted the money for himself. *"Not that he cared for the poor – he was a thief, and since he was in charge of the disciples' money, he often stole some for himself"* (John 12:6 NLT). Judas' comments stirred the other disciples and they began to speak harshly to Mary also (Mk 14:5-6).

Outcome

Judas betrayed the Lord. During the Last Supper he sat beside Jesus, took the bread and Satan entered him (John 13:27). Judas left and led the soldiers to Jesus. He later became convicted of his actions, but it was too late; he committed suicide. *"Then he threw down the pieces of silver in the temple and departed and went and hanged himself"* (Matt 27:5).

Saul and David

"So, the women sang as they danced, and said: 'Saul has slain his thousands, and David his ten thousands.'"

~ 1Samuel 18:7 NKJV

Offense

Initially Saul approved of David but after the women celebrated him for killing Goliath, he became jealous.

Motive

Saul was intimidated by the attention David received and the anointing upon his life. The song of the women stirred anger in Saul. He said, *"They have credited David with tens of thousands," he thought, "but me with only thousands. What more can he get but the kingdom?"* (1Sa 18:8 NIV).

Outcome

Saul tried to kill David many times. When David was given the opportunity to take revenge, he chose not to. Saul regretted his actions when he learned what David had done. *"Then he said to David: "You are more righteous than I; for you have rewarded me with good, whereas I have rewarded you with evil"* (1Sa 24:17 NKJV).

Jesus and the Syro-Phoenician Woman

"But Jesus said to her, "Let the children be filled first, for it is not good to take the children's bread and throw it to the little dogs."

~ Mark 7:27 NKJV

Offense

At this time, there was a lot of attention focused on Jesus because many had seen and heard of his teachings and miracles. Just as He planned to take time for a little rest, a foreign woman imposed. She was seeking help for her demon-possessed daughter. She came in, fell at his feet and begged for help. He responded to her by comparing her to a dog (Mk 7:27 NKJV).

Motive

The Greek word used in this statement is *"kunarion"* (koo-nar'-ee-on), which refers to a household pet. Therefore, Jesus used this term to test the sincerity of the Gentile woman's faith.

Outcome

She could have taken offense, but she chose to stand firm in her purpose: deliverance for her daughter. Instead of taking offense this woman pursued Jesus' favor. He met her at her place of need.

Other biblical examples:

Adam – Genesis 3
Jonah – Jonah 3 & 4
Moses and the Israelites – Exodus 14:10-12
Miriam and Aaron – Numbers 12
John the Baptist – Matthew 11:4-6
Jesus – Mark 9:19; 11:12-14

Chapter 15
A Treasury of Testimonies

"And they overcame him by the blood of the Lamb and by the word of their testimony, and they did not love their lives to the death."

~ Revelation 12:11 NKJV

Offense happens to all of us and when it does, it may seem as if no one understands, or has experienced the same type of situation. Emotionally, this perception appears to be correct, but it isn't. According to John the Revelator, when we share our testimony of what the Lord has done in our lives, we are strengthened to overcome anything. This authority is activated when believers exercise their covenant rights. It is because of the shed blood of Jesus that the Believer has victory over offense. The blood gives us power. Through the blood of Jesus, we don't have to stand on our own, we stand in the power of God. No matter what we try to do, righteousness is found in Christ. We are rescued out of sin. The blood provides salvation of our souls, forgiveness from sins, access to God, victory over the enemy, and the power to live with a clear conscience. Hebrews 9:14 says, *"...how much more will the blood of Christ, who through the eternal Spirit offered himself without blemish to God, purifying our conscience from dead works to serve the living God"* (NKJV). Walking in offense is a dead work, but the blood empowers us through our living faith, to think and live right according to God's plan and His Word.

Our faith in God and what He can do is increased when we tell what the Lord has done and what He is doing in our lives right now. The more we lift His name, the more we testify, the more real He becomes to you and the more powerful you become.

Testimony 1

I am the president of a new chapter of a national organization. According to procedures, I am required to notify the Headquarters by a certain date, with a listing of members who complied with all local and national requirements under the President's seal, in order to permanently identify the charter (founding) members. One of the charter organizers, who was known to faithfully contribute his time, talents and energy, failed to meet the local financial contribution by two weeks. Ordinarily, he was current. The vice president, treasurer, secretary and I, all offered to help him pay the dues, but he stated, "I got it."

Two months after the due date, we held a large public event with the local, state and national hierarchy members present. During the event, only the charter brothers were acknowledged, as called for by protocol of the event. Two days later, this member contacted the top four leaders and stated I had offended him by not forwarding his overdue contribution, even though he failed to meet his obligation. I admit that it stumbled me, and I prayed to God that I would find a fair resolution to his dilemma yet be cognizant not to open Pandora's box---there were several other members who would be eligible too by the criteria this member requested. I also thought about the people who followed the mandate and made sacrifices for the financial contribution on time, regardless.

As I consulted with the three other senior leaders, I was shown evidence, in digital form, proving without a doubt that the member had a timely notice of his financial obligation. For whatever reason, he overlooked the payment until he recognized the value in being named a charter member on the founding document. I sought private time with the member by offering to meet with him at a well-known restaurant to discuss the quandary. Via text I was told, there was nothing to talk about unless the founders document could be modified to add his name. Unfortunately, his friends chose to honor him as a founder although he failed to comply with the rules.

I thought about it again overnight and informed the member that although I could have the charter document changed, as president, I would do so for the principle of unity and only with the unanimous approval of the local organization. I learned that God was teaching me that leaders are to walk in patience and fairness, while maintaining impartiality and Godly love. This resolved the issue of offense within me.

~ Douglas A. Young, Lieutenant Colonel, US Air Force (Retired)
& Business Manager Tom Bush BMW of Orange Park
Fleming Island, Fl.

Testimony 2

Growing up and singing in a gospel choir right out of college, I was one of the lead singers on the choir, and one of the younger choir members. Most of the songs I sang were upbeat and "fresh." Our choir was going on tour in New York. The director had given out almost all the solos. They were all new "popping" music. When it was time to give me a song, she gave me this old-time negro spiritual. It was one of those songs that you would envision an older "Mahalia Jackson" type of woman to be singing. I was angry. I felt I was much too young to be singing that song. I was a little hurt that she gave me the "worst" song to sing in the entire line-up. To make matters worse, I didn't even like the song! I felt like it should have been given to an older person to sing.

Reluctantly, I prepared to minister the song. During the first concert, much to my surprise, the song I sang came over very, very well. Many people were blessed by it. What this taught me is, obedience is better than sacrifice. When we take ourselves out of the picture, and let God take control, things will work out for the good. It also taught me that as a singer, sometimes the blessing is for the receiver and not the giver.

~ Jacqueline Moss
President Jacqueline Moss Insurance Agency
CEO of Snatcher Inc
Charlotte, NC

Testimony 3

My offense came in a work situation. I was assigned to the Project Management department as a Project Management Associate. I had worked in the department for two years and was very competent in what my duties were. All the information system projects that I was assigned to get implemented were completed without any failure. We hired another project associate who had completed his certification and was new to the field. I was assigned as his mentor with the responsibility of training him. After three months, a position for a Project Manager came open. I was the senior associate. Within days, the position was given to the new guy. What is worse, I was told to teach him everything I knew about project management. Essentially, I was now working for him. My credentials, work experience, and past results made me the best candidate for the position, and I was very hurt that I wasn't even considered or given the opportunity to interview for the position. After working for an additional two months and recognizing how challenged and incapable the new guy was, I decided to leave the agency. I was doing all the work and he was getting all the credit. It caused me to question my value.

This situation taught me to be more proactive, to know my worth and confront the offender when I feel that I am offended. I am a better person now and my trajectory has been enhanced since I've taken control of my career.

~ Anthony Minter
Senior Auditor
Columbia, SC
Pastor of True Believers Church & Ministries

Testimony 4

After starting a business years ago, I shared with a friend some difficulties I was having with my company. Unfortunately, the response was not positive. I was shocked and offended by the words: "You should go work for a company." The person I thought supported me, did not believe I could be successful." Despite the negative comment, I chose to prove to myself…I am good enough! I jumped all in, and became a successful entrepreneur, author, and motivational speaker. My mission is to encourage, enrich, and empower others to achieve their goals. Note to self...

"Let the offenses of others become the motivating fuel needed to create the successful life you desire."

~ Jadon Y. Connor, CPC
Knect6, Founder and Marketing Director
Charlotte, NC

Testimony 5

One evening, a friend and I had made last minute plans to celebrate the New Year. She and I had decided to go to an event together. Unbeknownst to me, shortly after that discussion, she had made plans for the same event with others and excluded me. I arrived at the facility and could not get in touch with her. She did not answer my call or return my text. I waited for about 15 minutes before leaving. I was upset. I thought of how I would never have done her this way. I thought of the times that I included her in activities with my other groups of friends. However, I did not allow those emotions to consume me. She reached out to me days later about something unrelated. She never acknowledged what happened that New Year's Eve. I wanted to ignore her message, but I didn't. I wanted to confront her, and I chose not to. I was hurt by what my friend had done to me. I didn't discuss it with her at all. Later, when I did consider discussing it, my sister suggested that I shouldn't say anything at the time. I thought that I wouldn't get an honest answer and it wasn't worth the trouble. After some time passed, at the advice of my little sister, I briefly engaged in conversation. My positive reaction allowed me to maintain peace.

I decided to move past that moment, but make it a teachable one. God was teaching me to practice peace and avoid unnecessary negative situations as much as possible. I still have a relationship with my friend, and she doesn't know how I felt about the situation. I have forgiven her, but I have changed how I deal with her. I no longer feel obligated to participate if I am not interested or include her if she was not a part of the original plan. Now, I politely respond, "No, I'm not going to make it" or "I already have plans."

~ Karina Liles, PhD
Assistant Professor of Computer Science
Columbia, SC

Testimony 6

When people say I do not mean to offend you that means they are getting ready to say something that can be interpreted as an offense. As wives, we tend to believe that our spouses should act according to what we believe and not necessarily what the Bible teaches. I believe this is because we grow up seeing different things. Looking at different television shows influences how we think. In addition, it does not help when we do not seek Godly counsel, such as premarital counsel. We tend to make declarations without having conversations with our spouses. My husband and I were both young and had no Godly examples of marriage, so we struggled with our marital relationship. In addition, we both came from very different homes. For example, once my husband had to go out of town and he asked me to deliver his child support payment to the woman he had previously had an affair with. I agreed to do so. Later after I got home, he began to tell me things she had said about me. We ended up arguing and I became offended. I was his wife, she was the "other woman," and being questioned for trying to do the right thing did not sit well with me at all. The fact that he came home and questioned me was not the problem, but the fact that he questioned me concerning what the "other woman" had said was truly offensive. I felt that he had chosen another side and it was not the side of his family.

At the time, in my mind, I feared that my husband would leave me. I had always felt he would leave, and this is what was looming in my mind at the time and it did not help. Ironically, I was the one people would call the strong, independent, black woman, as my mother would say. She encouraged me to get my education, a good job, and to own my own home without being dependent upon a man – to get my own money as she put it. I entered our marriage with this disposition. I really needed the Holy Spirit to work with me to get my mind right, according to the Word of God. I went through some hard places because of my disposition, but it was truly in those hard places that I allowed the Spirit of the Lord to shape my thinking. In these experiences, I realized that God had my best interest at heart, and the only way I was going to have peace was if I allowed the Holy Spirit to minister to my broken heart and troubled mind.

My reception of the Holy Spirit brought healing and recovery of all the enemy thought he had stolen from my husband, our children, our marriage, and me. God has restored it all and I am unable to tell it all!

Working out this offense taught me to separate how I felt about a situation from what the Word of God says. Also, the Holy Spirit encouraged me to come to The Throne for twice: once for my natural husband and once for my spiritual husband, who is Christ. This principle has saved me so much additional pain, so I still implement this method when I want or need anything. God is truly my first husband. To God Be the Glory!

~ Mary Hancock, EdD.
Financial Educator
Author of *I'm Screaming: Can You Hear Me?* and *What to Do When*
Irmo, SC

Testimony 7

My husband was recently promoted to the position of director on his job. This means that the men he used to work with as teammates, he is now their managing director and they report to him. He now supervises employees that were formerly his colleagues. My husband is black and the other three supervisors are white. (This should not make a difference, but it does.) As he explained, there were a few vehicles that had been out of the fleet for a while, so last Thursday he asked the company mechanic about them and why they had not been repaired. As he explained it to me, my husband approached the fleet manager and requested a repair status on a few company vehicles that had been inoperable for several weeks. Instead of answering the question the mechanic responded, "These guys don't do their jobs around here!" My husband then asked, "Well if you're a supervisor, why haven't you addressed the work ethic issue with the staff in question?"

The mechanic replied, "Marvin, I'm not gonna tell a black man that he's not doing his job." I typically don't fall out emotionally about the "race" issue. But when my husband came home and told me about it, I was enraged! I demanded that he be prosecuted to the fullest extent of the law; take legal action; and have the man fired! This particular person keeps antagonizing my husband and resisting his authority. I was hurt for him and I "went off." The Lord allowed me to vent and when I was done, I could hear Him ask, "Are you finished?"

From there, I went into prayer and read the Word. God showed me myself - as usual! One passage of Scripture God laid on my heart is Matthew 5:38-40; I am to show mercy to others because I am in such great need of the same!

~ Aronissa Harris
Minister & Financial Consultant
Philadelphia, PA

Testimony 8

I recall a time when I was very offended because I was attempting to work through a challenge I was having with a family member, and the response I received was very nonchalant and seemingly uncaring. I felt I wasn't being heard and my thoughts and feelings weren't important, which created a myriad of emotions including rejection, defensiveness, sadness and hurt feelings.

I remember going to church after dropping my children off at school the next morning and laying on the altar. Quite frankly, I was having a pity party that I called prayer. I looked up at some point and I saw something that looked wrong with the baseboard on the pulpit. In the midst of crying my eyes out, this 'thing' caught my attention and as I studied it, it looked as if a piece of the baseboard had actually come off. I got up from the floor and walked to take a closer look and I saw a church program had fallen down and perfectly lined up with the rest of the baseboard creating an image of something that it was not. It was at that moment that I heard The Lord say, "Everything ISN'T what it seems."

I was floored as I listened to Him talk me through my array of emotions. He let me know that the Spirit of Offense had lied to me. Because of my thoughts and feelings of how someone should act or respond to the circumstance and because I heard what was said from my viewpoint only, I was a wounded mess... a victim of offense, which was sending me to a place where this relationship could have had fatal consequences. Offense is designed to kill! It is a strategic tactic of the enemy and it threw me off and out of place until The Spirit of Truth showed up.

As a result of that experience and lesson well over 10 years ago, I've learned that indeed everything isn't what it seems. Offense opens a door for the enemy to try and uproot harmony among other things, but I've learned to assess life's situations from a sober, non-emotional viewpoint and not allow my emotions or thoughts to take me on a journey outside of truth.

~ Monya Grant, MBA
Prophetess
Rivers of Living Water International, Chicago, IL

Testimony 9

I once believed that it was impossible to develop true friends in your adult life. This is not to include a husband or wife, but genuine friends that were like your best friend from elementary school. As an adult, it seemed that friends came with conditions (often unspoken) and the minute you are unable to deliver on the expectations of the friendship the "friends" fade into the darkness or they react negatively to any disappointment.

Over 14 years ago, I met a gregarious young lady and we instantly became friends. Her personality was quite refreshing and contagious. We shared many common interests and formed a bond of sisterhood that was unmatched, so I thought. Our husbands knew one another from community involvement, our kids were close in age therefore fun times were on the rise. I don't have a biological sister, but can imagine that our relationship was similar to such. We shared tears of joy and pain, sunshine and rain. We talked on our ride to work most days to wish each other well. It was this friendship that made me think that I'd been wrong about previous thoughts on adult friendships.

After approximately four years of solid friendship, my spiritual gift of discernment kicked in and God revealed to me a distributing situation involving my great friend and others for which I had deep admiration. I made an attempt to help my friend navigate through the situation, but she was not willing to abandon it at the time. At this point, I knew that it was necessary for me to abandon the friendship. I did not wish to be associated with such a situation that had the potential to negatively impact hundreds of people.

I felt extremely betrayed by this friendship/sisterhood for so many reasons. Lies and deceit were at a high level. I recall framing my feelings by saying, "I've been played like a radio." I was utilized as a cover and a shield without my consent and knowledge.

In order to cope with feelings of hurt, disappointment and betrayal I had to face several truths:

1. Acceptance - I had to accept the fact that this person was not who I thought she was in terms of morals and values. That was not a reflection of our relationship. Understanding that we all make mistakes, we must STAND and RESPOND responsibly when we do.
2. Responsibility - I cannot be responsible for the actions of others. I wanted to force a change in the situation to make everything alright. I did not have the power to do so. I wanted my friendship back in tact and most of all I wanted my friend to be who I always thought she was. Finally, I had to continue to pray and let go.
3. Reality - My reality was that I should not take the situation personally. I had to come to terms that this undesirable

situation was not created for my destruction, it was created by two consenting adults for their personal gain.

Through acceptance, responsibility, and reality, today we have an acquaintanceship not a friendship and I wish them well. Most importantly, our God is forgiving, and I strive to live for Him. All is forgiven.

~ Sharon R. Earle, EdD.
Educator & Entrepreneur
Columbia, SC

Testimony 10

I serve as the Family Pastor and Counselor in Residence in a large church in suburban Atlanta. In 2016, we had four young ministers leave staff within a couple of months of one another. They were disgruntled with a lack of relationship with the Senior Pastor. As it happens, all of them, as they were evaluating their situation and deciding to leave or stay, came seeking my counsel at least once. As the church counselor, I support the staff as well as the congregants. Because they all resigned in close succession, the entire ordeal took on a conspiratorial air. The conclusion was drawn by the Senior Pastor and others on the church's executive leadership team that since they all came to see me, I must have encouraged all of them to leave.

The nature of my work as a therapist is cloaked in anonymity and confidentiality. Therefore, I do not volunteer information as to who comes to see me and who does not. However, due to the nature of this situation, I created a composite synopsis of my interactions with the ministers, making sure to preserve confidentiality and anonymity. My role was that of a listening ear, encouragement to pray on the issue of leaving staff and an exhortation that if they did decide to leave, they should let the Senior Pastor know why. Unfortunately, none of them did. I let my supervisor know the nature of the conversations. Whether that information was delivered to the remainder of the executive team remains a mystery to this day.

The offense within this situation has three prongs: 1) The erroneous conclusion that I encouraged them to leave the ministry staff. 2) No Senior Leadership bothered to ask me directly about the situation. 3) I was not provided better cover by my direct supervisor regarding this very sensitive matter. The matter was finally cleared up in 2019 during a meeting I had with the Senior Pastor. I told him exactly what I told each of those men. The Senior Pastor did not ask for forgiveness. The resolution for me was to address what had happened and forgive all involved in the offense. My forgiveness was important to God and my emotional wellbeing. I knew that unforgiveness weighs down the person that has not forgiven. I processed the pain of this wound for three years before I could finally forgive. That forgiveness released me.

~ Mel Turner, M.Div.
Family Pastor & Marriage Counselor
Stockbridge, GA

Testimony 11

As a therapist, the best methodology I offer to clients in mending a friendship is giving a genuine apology to clean up your side of the broken relationship. When it comes to repairing the connection, it is important to notice the pattern or patterns that caused the disruption or break in the relationship. After thoughtful reflection on why the friendship ended: a hurtful betrayal; a slow process of growing apart; a total misunderstanding, you can begin the process of seeking forgiveness. Furthermore, if possible, identify what life changes have occurred since the falling out. Recognizing the reasons you grew apart and how things might be different, you can now take the steps needed to rebuild a closer and longer lasting bond.

Reach out to your friend with an open heart to take the steps to reconnect. If the friend is not yet willing, do not be assertive or disrespectful. Trust is hard to earn once it is broken. But when you give the apology you must acknowledge what you did wrong, then give the reasons why you did what you did to help the other person understand your actions. As you continue conversation, give the wounded friend an opportunity to voice whatever feelings have arisen. This may be a long process depending on the severity of the disagreement and what you want to do with good and bad memories.

One key element to finding peace, understanding, and clarity is to not dwell on past mistakes so the relationship can move forward with new positive patterns. It is important to find common ground, to put your relationship ahead of your differences and to not let the past be reviewed in a blaming, negative manner. From this place of healing, you can have a new start and a build on that friendship lost with genuine love, trust and respect for one another.

For me personally, I was beyond hurt when accused of hurting not only my friend, but her mom. To think someone I considered a friend would accuse me of such an act cut to the core. What was supposed to be such a wonderful event in her life became a nightmare for our relationship. Why would someone place such a dark cloud on her wedding week with vicious lies? But why would she believe them and accuse me without giving me and our friendship more value.

I remember some of the phone calls that day that tore our friendship apart for years… the accusation and my anger. Surely my words were most inappropriate in lashing out, but my hurt and anger definitely felt justified. I couldn't believe this was happening to me again – not another friend accusing me of something that I absolutely had no idea of what was going on. My only thought was "how could she think I would hurt her and even worse her mother?"

For years, I wondered who poisoned my friend against me. But then I realized it wasn't about them it was more about my friend receiving the gossip. It didn't make me angry at our Judas, but more disappointed in my friend. Then life happened with so many highs and lows and the introduction of social media and there was my friend. So many years gone and events we could have shared together, and all feelings came flooding back. But not disappointment in her anymore, because through my self-awareness, I have had to be accountable and apologize to friends. No, I felt a deep sadness and longing for what could have been.

And then… I thank God she reached out and we talked. Even though our conversation seemed genuine, I must admit it wasn't until she came to my home that I truly felt the reconnection. Yes, it touched my heart to hear what transpired so many years ago and those simple three words, "I am sorry." But more than that, I truly felt her pain of the betrayal that severed our friendship. And to see and hug her and know she missed *us* as much as I had was restorative. Our reunion was bittersweet sharing memories and trying to recapture the years. Since this time, we've talked more and made promises to do better…now we need to honor our renewed friendship.

Regardless of the years we can't retrieve, I want my friend's heart free and clear. If not, we give the enemy that power which almost destroyed us. I love my friend and truly our bond now is forever.

~ Kimberly M. Hall, MBA, LMFT
ReVive Counseling
Charlotte, NC

Chapter 16
Scripture Tools

"For You will light my lamp; the Lord my God will enlighten my darkness."

~ Psalm 18:28 NJV

When you want to retaliate…

"You shall not take vengeance, nor bear any grudge against the children of your people, but you shall love your neighbor as yourself: I am the LORD."

~ Leviticus 19:18 NKJV

When you need strength…

"In return for my love they are my accusers, but I give myself to prayer."

~ Psalms 109:4 NKJV

When you struggle to please God…

"These six things the Lord hates, yes, seven are an abomination to Him: A proud look, a lying tongue, Hands that shed innocent blood, a heart that devises wicked plans, Feet that are swift in running to evil, a false witness who speaks lies, And one who sows discord among brethren."

~ Proverbs 6:16-19 NKJV

When you desire to keep peace…

"He who covers a transgression seeks love, but he who repeats a matter separates friends."

~ Proverbs 17:9 NKJV

When you need patience to wait…

"Rest in the LORD, and wait patiently for Him; Do not fret because of him who prospers in his way, because of the man who brings wicked schemes to pass. Cease from anger, and forsake wrath; do not fret—it only causes harm. For evildoers shall be cut off; but those who wait on the Lord, they shall inherit the earth."

~ Psalm 37:7-9 NKJV

When you need wisdom…

"He who is devoid of wisdom despises his neighbor, but a man of understanding holds his peace."

~ Proverbs 11:12 NKJV

When you need instruction…

"Open rebuke is better than love carefully concealed. Faithful are the wounds of a friend, but the kisses of an enemy are deceitful."

~Proverbs 27:5-6 NKJV

When people talk about you…

"Do not pay attention to every word people say, or you may hear your servant cursing you — for you know in your heart that many times you yourself have cursed others."

Ecclesiastes 7:21-22 NKJV

When you need hope...

> "He shall see the labor of His soul, and be satisfied. By His knowledge, My righteous Servant shall justify many, for He shall bear their iniquities."
>
> ~ Isaiah 53:11 NKJV

When you need courage for the task...

> "Therefore, my beloved brethren, be steadfast, immovable, always abounding in the work of the Lord, knowing that your labor is not in vain in the Lord."
>
> ~ 1Corinthians 15:58 NKJV

When you should pray for your offender...

> "Woe to the world because of offenses! For offenses must come, but woe to that man by whom the offense comes!"
>
> ~ Matthew 18:7 NKJV

When you are feeling discouraged...

> "Trust in the LORD with all your heart, and lean not on your own understanding; in all your ways acknowledge Him, and He shall direct your paths."
>
> ~ Proverbs 3:5-6 NKJV

When you are prideful...

> "Take heed to yourselves. If your brother sins against you, rebuke him; and if he repents, forgive him. And if he sins against you seven times in a day, and seven times in a day returns to you, saying, 'I repent,' you shall forgive him."
>
> ~ Luke 17:3-4 NKJV

When your faith needs stirring…

> *"This being so, I myself always strive to have a conscience without offense toward God and men."*
>
> ~ Acts 24:16 NKJV

When you need God's assurance…

> *"Therefore, I take pleasure in infirmities, in reproaches, in needs, in persecutions, in distresses, for Christ's sake. For when I am weak, then I am strong."*
>
> ~ 2Corinthians 12:10 NKJV

When you are justifying your pain…

> *"I have been crucified with Christ; it is no longer I who live, but Christ lives in me; and the life which I now live in the flesh I live by faith in the Son of God, who loved me and gave Himself for me."*
>
> ~ Galatians 2:20 NKJV

When you have sinned…

> *"For you, brethren, have been called to liberty; only do not use liberty as an opportunity for the flesh, but through love serve one another."*
>
> ~ Galatians 5:13 NKJV

When you need to get along with others…

> *"With all lowliness and gentleness, with longsuffering, bearing with one another in love, endeavoring to keep the unity of the Spirit in the bond of peace."*
>
> ~ Ephesians 4:2-3 NKJV

When you need help to forgive...

> *"And be kind to one another, tenderhearted, forgiving one another, even as God in Christ forgave you."*
>
> ~ Ephesians 4:32 NKJV

When you have the opportunity to demonstrate good character...

> *"And a servant of the Lord must not quarrel but be gentle to all, able to teach, patient."*
>
> ~ 2Timothy 2:24 NKJV

When you feel down and out...

> *Now no chastening seems to be joyful for the present, but painful; nevertheless, afterward it yields the peaceable fruit of righteousness to those who have been trained by it."*
>
> ~ Hebrews 12:11 NKJV

When you want to be fruitful...

> *"Blessed is the man Who walks not in the counsel of the ungodly, nor stands in the path of sinners, nor sits in the seat of the scornful; but his delight is in the law of the Lord, and in His law he meditates day and night. He shall be like a tree planted by the rivers of water, that brings forth its fruit in its season, whose leaf also shall not wither; and whatever he does shall prosper.*
>
> ~ Psalm 1:1-3 NKJV

When you are tempted...

> *"Who, when He was reviled, did not revile in return; when He suffered, He did not threaten, but committed Himself to Him who judges righteously."*
>
> ~ 1Peter 2:23 NKJV

When adversity is overwhelming…

> *"If you are reproached for the name of Christ, blessed are you, for the Spirit of glory and of God rests upon you. On their part He is blasphemed, but on your part, He is glorified."*
>
> ~ 1Peter 4:14 NKJV

When you need the secret to loving without offense…

> *"Therefore, as the elect of God, holy and beloved, put on tender mercies, kindness, humility, meekness, longsuffering; bearing with one another, and forgiving one another, if anyone has a complaint against another; even as Christ forgave you, so you also must do. But above all these things put on love, which is the bond of perfection. And let the peace of God rule in your hearts, to which also you were called in one body; and be thankful. Let the word of Christ dwell in you richly in all wisdom, teaching and admonishing one another in psalms and hymns and spiritual songs, singing with grace in your hearts to the Lord. And whatever you do in word or deed, do all in the name of the Lord Jesus, giving thanks to God the Father through Him."*
>
> ~ Colossians 3:12-17 NKJV

Afterword

The increase of offense is partially due to the absence of knowledge and intimacy with the Lord. By definition of who you are in Christ, the actions of others should not have the power to induce "petty pain" in your life. You must stop and think about who you are, and what is underneath your negative feelings about what has been said or done. This is how you take authority over the situation. You do not have to settle for less than God's best in your life. Living with "petty pain" can potentially destroy your relationships with those you love the most. It has the power to affect the marital bond, the parent/child relationship, the workplace, social circles and the church.

The topic of offense is one of the most neglected areas in the life of believers, yet it is continuing to be one of the most difficult areas to overcome. This lack of attention has created a stronger resistance in the souls of those who walk in offense. It has become the way their lives are framed. Unfortunately, this toxic perspective can shake the foundation of people's lives, whether saved or unsaved. The Hebrews writer suggested there will come a time when the Lord will shake heaven and earth until the only things that can remain are those things which cannot be shaken (Heb 12:27). Shaking is significant because it is a method used to separate or pull apart one thing from another. The people of God are often attached to things that God is trying to rid them of, so spiritual separation becomes necessary for the purpose of growth, maturity, and testimony.

I like to relate spiritual separation with the threshing process. The threshing floor is an elevated platform where harvested wheat is taken so that the outer layer of the grain can be removed. Before the harvest, the chaff has served its purpose, which is to provide a covering for the grain as it matures. The threshing process pulls apart the worthless chaff from the valuable grain kernel. After the wheat has been beaten and stomped, the grain kernel is exposed, but it takes the wind to separate the chaff from the grain. The harvester then throws the wheat and chaff in the air together and the valuable grain kernel falls to the floor as the wind blows away the worthless chaff.

Many times in life, the value of a process is missed because people reject the pressure of the impact, or the beating. To harness the value of the force, it requires that you give-in to the painful process, this is where the issues of the heart - grain kernel - are revealed. Proverbs 23:26 says, *"My son, give me your heart, and let your eyes observe my ways"* (NKJV). This is an invitation to grow closer to God. Relationships have the power to influence our lives. As your knowledge of God increases so should your desire to please Him. A wounded and offended heart struggles with obedience, but a pure heart will yield to the Holy Spirit. Make no mistake, the Lord is always looking to transform your life by changing your mind and purifying the heart. If a believer is not secure in his spiritual identity in Christ, he will allow his heart to be walled in by insecurities, shame, betrayal, anger, embarrassment, pride and ignorance.

God allows offenses to happen to shake you free from anything that has been clinging to the heart. Like the grain kernel, the heart is the most valuable part of man. Therefore, Christians have a duty to seek God's wisdom whenever you feel offended. In the shaking and looking, God reveals what needs to be removed so that you can grow and mature. If left unchecked, your lives will no longer resemble the character of Christ, but they will look more like the world. This crafty work of Satan is very successful in ruining your witness, both inside and outside the church. It is not God's will that we walk in offense. Make the decision to accept that offense is a part of life and you do not have to accept it. If you have accepted Satan's assignment, you can overcome it through Christ.

Let us nail offense to the cross by releasing our petty pain to the Lord.

~ **Margo W. Williams**

Appendix A

Cycle of Offense

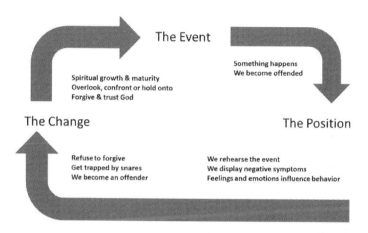

If we walk around being offended by the words or actions of others, our own progress is hindered. The enemy sets a snare in our path to trap us. This is designed to lead us astray with the purpose of destroying our witness. Once we get intimate with the Spirit of Offense, we begin to invite his family members into our hearts. The closest members are pride, unforgiveness, and vengeance. Once they come to visit, in a twisted way, we lose the power and integrity to tell them to leave. Why? When we need them to make us feel powerful and justified, pride, unforgiveness and vengeance are faithful and loyal companions. By this time, unaware of what we have done, we have revealed how sinful we really are. Sadly, we have truly misrepresented Christ and we are still justifying our feelings. The irony is that the one who started out as being offended has now become the offender. Each time we share our justifiable reason for "being the way I am," in the attempt to sway people against our offenders, we have caused many to stumble. We are living hypocritically since we confess one thing while living another. All the while, Satan is happy because the purposes of God are being hampered.

Where we were making progress, one offensive act or word has divided the hearts of families, friends, homes and churches.

Appendix B

Survey Questions

"Father, I ask you to deal with my heart and mind right now. I am aware of the enemy's tactics and I declare that he shall not prosper over me. You have given me the mind of Christ and He is welcome to invade my thoughts, will and emotions. I recognize that You are the discerner of the heart and mind and I ask You to search my heart and show me myself. Reveal to me where I am offended and help me to forgive all I have been unable or unwilling to forgive. I ask Your Spirit to enable and teach me to walk as Jesus did. Lord, please remove every wall and judgment I have within me. I ask You for more grace. In Jesus name. Amen."

Circle the correct answer.

1.	When someone says/does something that bothers me, I take it personally.	Y/N
2.	It bothers me to be around a person who has hurt my feelings.	Y/N
3.	I believe I know other's intentions when something is said/done against me.	Y/N
4.	Once I let someone know how I feel, I forgive easily and demonstrate mercy.	Y/N
5.	I have friends/relatives/co-workers that I no longer speak to or give a "cold" shoulder.	Y/N
6.	Once I feel betrayed by someone, I have nothing else to do with him/her.	Y/N

7.	I can name at least one time in my life I was rejected by someone I love.	Y/N
8.	I justify why I am right (righteous) and condemn others as being in sin.	Y/N
9.	Even when wronged, I can bless the one who hurt me and sincerely mean it.	Y/N
10.	When I have been hurt/betrayed by someone I love, I repeatedly think about how I feel.	Y/N
11.	Growing up, in my family I saw examples of affection, discipline, forgiveness, and love.	Y/N
12.	I do not understand why I "cut people off" when I see them, but I have forgiven them.	Y/N
13.	I pick and choose who I want to be "warm" with so it's clear that "I'm not playing" with someone who I do not like, trust, or care for.	Y/N
14.	I am very aware of my "self-concerns" (Who was rude to me. When my feelings got hurt. Who disrespected me.)	Y/N
15.	I expect others, especially spiritual leaders to be perfect knowing that I am not.	Y/N
16.	I have changed churches because of being hurt by the pastor, leaders, or the teachings.	Y/N
17.	I understand the difference in suspicion and discernment.	Y/N
18.	When emotional I can still discern the voice of God.	Y/N
19.	Some ways I have are "just the way I am" and I do not expect them to change.	Y/N
20.	When I am justifying myself, I confidently declare "God knows my heart."	Y/N
	Based on your answers, do you believe you are walking in offense?	Y/N

With help from the Holy Spirit, you can forgive your offender(s) and be freed from the trap of offense.

Appendix C

Triunity of Man

Now may the God of peace make you holy in every way, and may your whole spirit and soul and body be kept blameless until our Lord Jesus Christ comes again.
1Thess 5:23 NLT

SPIRIT	SOUL	BODY
Inner Core	Personality	External Shell
"Ruah"	"Nephesh"	"sarx"
Isaiah 11:2	Genesis 2:7	Romans 12:1-2
Proverbs 20:27	Ephesians 4:23	
	James 1:21	
Communication with God		5 Senses
Salvation		Action
Acceptance & Assurance	Mind	Speech
Love	Will	Logic
Wisdom & Understanding	Emotions	Intuition
Counsel	Relates to Others	Relates to the Environment
Power	Conscious Mind	Conscious Mind
Knowledge	Sub-conscious Mind	Sub-conscious Mind
Grace		

You are a SPIRIT
You have a SOUL
You live in a BODY

When we have a solid understanding of our triune nature, we become powerful instruments in the Hand of God. When we are born-again, our spirit is renewed or becomes brand new. The new spirit houses the indwelling presence of the Holy Spirit within the believer. Both the body and the soul has to be renewed to the change made in the spirit. Prior to salvation, the soul operated according to how it felt and reasoned and the body obeyed. The Apostle Paul says that we are to *"be transformed by the renewing of your mind, that you may prove what is that good and acceptable and perfect will of God"* (Rom 12:2). First, the mind must change. Second, it's your responsibility to prove your change to God. When we prove something it means that we have erased doubt by showing something to be true. Although our transformation is a process, we are to be processing the change through the process of sanctification.

When the mind hasn't been renewed to the Word of God we allow ourselves to be governed by the soul rather than the spirit. Satan understands this and uses it to his advantage. As we come into proper alignment with God's Word more power is released into our lives. Think of it this way: Prior to being born-again the soul acts as a "switchboard" for your life and it has to be reprogrammed. Instead of the body responding to signals from the soul, now the spirit becomes the switchboard and the Holy Spirit becomes the operator.

The soul is the most vulnerable part of man, so Satan attacks the central place of our being. This is the place the enemy works to if you struggle with feelings of The Spirit of Offense is a housed within the soul.

Appendix D

Confessions

You are the God who pardons.

I am the righteousness of God.

I am Your child and I commit to walk in the love of God.

I am growing in my faith in God.

I speak words that bring honor and glory to Your name.

I endure long and I am patient and kind as I wait.

I take no account of evil done to me.

I stand ready to think and believe the best of others.

I walk in the Spirit; therefore, I am not easily offended.

I carry the fruit of the Spirit.

You are my joy and strength.

If my brother offends me, I will forgive him up to seventy times seven.

I refuse to allow Satan to occupy or influence my words, emotions, or behaviors.

Your Word is planted deeply within my heart.

I have been delivered from the power of darkness into the Light.

I cast my cares upon You.

I lay aside the weight of fear, anxiety, rejection, low self-esteem, wrath, _____.

I am a hearer and doer of Your word.

I walk in the wisdom of God.

I am strong in the Lord and the power of His might.

I resist temptation for evil thoughts, words and deeds.

My motives are pure and righteous.

I judge not, and I shall not be judged. I condemn not and shall not be condemned.

I confess _____ (name your sin), You are faithful to forgive me of _____ (named sin), and to cleanse me from all unrighteousness.

Appendix E

Petty Pain Blockers

"The anger of a fool becomes readily apparent, but the prudent person overlooks an insult."

~ Proverbs 12:16 ISV

Practice Patience

"Sensible people control their temper; they earn respect by overlooking wrongs."

~ Proverbs 19:11 NIV

"People with understanding control their anger; a hot temper shows great foolishness."

~ Proverbs 14:29 NLT

Watch Your Words

"He was oppressed and treated harshly, yet he never said a word. He was led like a lamb to the slaughter. And as a sheep is silent before the shearers, he did not open his mouth."

~ Isaiah 53:7 NLT

"When they heaped abuse on Him, He did not retaliate; when He suffered, He made no threats, but entrusted Himself to Him who judges justly."

~ 1Peter 2:23 BSB

Seek Counsel

"The way of a fool is right in his own eyes, but he who heeds counsel is wise"

~ Proverbs 12:15 NKJV

Self-Inventory

"Why do you look at the speck that is in your brother's eye, but do not notice the log that is in your own eye? Or how can you say to your brother, 'Let me remove the speck from your eye'; and look, a plank is in your own eye? Hypocrite! First remove the plank from your own eye, and then you will see clearly to remove the speck from your brother's eye."

~ Matthew 7:3-5 NKJV

Look Beyond the Situation

"For our present troubles are small and won't last very long. Yet they produce for us a glory that vastly outweighs them and will last forever! So, we don't look at the troubles we can see now; rather, we fix our gaze on things that cannot be seen. For the things we see now will soon be gone, but the things we cannot see will last forever."

~ 2Corinthians 4:17-18 NLT

"Looking unto Jesus, the author and finisher of our faith, who for the joy that was set before Him endured the cross, despising the shame, and has sat down at the right hand of the throne of God. For consider Him who endured such hostility from sinners against Himself, lest you become weary and discouraged in your souls."

~ Hebrews 12:2-3 NKJV

Be a Peacemaker

"The work of righteousness will be peace; the service of righteousness will be quiet confidence forever."

~ Isaiah 32:17 BSB

"And those who are peacemakers will plant seeds of peace and reap a harvest of righteousness."

~ James 3:18 NLT

Exercise Genuine Love

"A new commandment I give to you, that you love one another; as I have loved you, that you also love one another."

~ John 13:34 NKJV

"You were cleansed from your sins when you obeyed the truth, so now you must show sincere love to each other as brothers and sisters. Love each other deeply with all your heart."

~ 1Peter 1:22 NLT

Appendix F

Prayers

Prayer of Release

Lord, I stand before You, recognizing that You are God and beside You there is no other. I call You God Almighty. I call you Strength. I call you Peace. I call You Redeemer. I magnify Your name. I adore You, Father. Your ways are better than life and I reverence You. Father, You said in Your Word that You are close to the brokenhearted and my heart has been hurting for a while. I confess that I struggle with doing what I know to be righteous and I do not want to struggle any longer. My heart needs mending and I need you right now. I have come to realize that I can't do this on my own. Lord, help me to do what I have not wanted to do in the past. I want to live in peace and have harmony with all people, even those who have hurt me.

I release myself from being offended and the Spirit of Offense. I give you my bitterness, resentment, envy, anger, and hostility. I shut off all thoughts, attitudes and voices that would influence me to hold onto the things You command that I let go of today. I am saying no to retaliation, criticizing others, judgmental thoughts and words. Lord, ask You to wash my heart, cleanse me with Your Word today. I yield myself to You – my mind, my will and my emotions. Have Your way in me. Please forgive me for allowing the enemy to have room in my heart and mind. Thank you for the mercy and grace You have given me.

I release those who have intended harm to me and those who never meant me any harm. I forgive my enemies, persecutors, critics and manipulators. I bless them. I love them. I ask You to forgive them and be merciful to them according to Your lovingkindness. As You open my eyes to see Truth, I ask that You open theirs also.

Father, I thank You that today I have forgiven, and I forgive. Even in the times that I am reminded of the petty pain of the past, I am trusting You to strengthen me. I won't look back because I am looking to You. I thank You that by Your Spirit, the precious Holy Spirit, I am walking in liberty, the freedom of forgiveness and the power of love. You have given me all that pertains to life and godliness and I walk in Your ways. I won't look around, but I will look to You, the One who leads, guides, teaches and heals me. Glory to Your name! Hallelujah! Father, I thank You for Your mercy and grace. Thank You for hearing my heart's cry and answering my prayer. In Jesus name. Amen.

Prayer of Salvation

Lord, I am coming to you knowing that I am a sinner and I want to be saved. I have tried so many things and nothing has worked. I am at the end of myself. I realize that I need You and I want to be saved. I am stepping out of my way and I am asking You to come into my heart. I ask You to fill the empty places in my heart, my mind and my will.

I believe and I confess that Jesus died for my sins. I confess that He was raised from the dead, and He is living in Heaven. I ask You today, right now, to be Lord of my life. I ask You, Holy Spirit, to help me to obey and trust You with my whole being. In Jesus name. Amen.

About the Author

Living a life that honors the Lord is a priority and motivation for Margo W. Williams. She is an educator, Christian Life Coach, chaplain, missionary, entrepreneur, and public speaker. Margo unselfishly uses her teaching and preaching gifts to transform and empower others to live in the authority of their salvation in Christ. Rev. Williams is passionate about worship, intercession, discipleship, healing and deliverance. Her call to the Nations has provided the opportunity for her to teach, preach and train leaders in Africa and India. She is also the co-founder of *The Master's Joy Discipleship Ministry*. She is a licensed and ordained minister and serves as an Associate at her local church. Margo has also earned a Master of Divinity degree from Columbia International University Seminary and School of Missions. Currently she is a doctoral candidate at Erskine Theological Seminary. She resides in Irmo, SC with her husband Lee and they have two adult children.

To contact Rev. Margo W. Williams
Write: PO Box 1361, Irmo SC 29063
Email: margoprazgodnow@gmail.com
Visit: www.margowwilliams.org

Graceful Fire Publishing is a ministry of
Margo W. Williams Ministries

Made in the USA
Columbia, SC
07 July 2020